Marion Milner

C000051097

This focused and thorough book by Alberto Stefana and Alessio Gamba delves into Marion Milner's contribution to psychoanalytic clinical theory and technique.

The authors offer an overview of Milner's work as a psychoanalyst, writer, and gifted painter. They bring to light how each of her clinical concepts and theorizations have been shaped by predecessors and, in turn, have inspired subsequent analysts. The importance of imaginative scenarios for both patient and therapist within the analytic context is particularly emphasized. The authors conclude by focusing on the retained clinical relevance of Milner's contribution for contemporary psychoanalysis. *Marion Milner: A Contemporary Introduction* is essential for students of psychoanalysis, as well as academics and psychoanalytic practitioners interested in the clinical-theoretical work of this pioneer in psychoanalysis.

Alberto Stefana serves as a psychotherapist for adolescents and adults in conjunction with his role as an academic researcher. He has published over 100 articles on clinical psychology, psychoanalysis, and psychiatry in international journals.

Alessio Gamba is a psychotherapist for children, adolescents, and couples. He worked in the developmental psychology unit and the neuropsychiatry clinic of San Gerardo Hospital in Monza, Italy and is currently an adjunct professor at the Milano-Bicocca University and at the ASNEA School of Specialization in Psychotherapy in Monza.

Routledge Introductions to Contemporary Psychoanalysis

Aner Govrin, Ph.D.
Series Editor

Yael Peri Herzovich, Ph.D.
Executive Editor

Itamar Ezer
Assistant Editor

Routledge Introductions to Contemporary Psychoanalysis is one of the prominent psychoanalytic publishing ventures of our day. It will comprise dozens of books that will serve as concise introductions dedicated to influential concepts, theories, leading figures, and techniques in psychoanalysis covering every important aspect of psychoanalysis. The length of each book is fixed at 40,000 words.

The series' books are designed to be easily accessible to provide informative answers in various areas of psychoanalytic thought. Each book will provide updated ideas on topics relevant to contemporary psychoanalysis – from the unconscious and dreams, projective identification and eating disorders, through neuropsychoanalysis, colonialism, and spiritual-sensitive psychoanalysis. Books will also be dedicated to prominent figures in the field, such as Melanie Klein, Jaque Lacan, Sandor Ferenczi, Otto Kernberg, and Michael Eigen.

Not serving solely as an introduction for beginners, the purpose of the series is to offer compendiums of information on particular topics within different psychoanalytic schools. We ask authors to review a topic but also address the readers with their own personal views and contribution to the specific chosen field. Books will make intricate ideas comprehensible without compromising their complexity.

We aim to make contemporary psychoanalysis more accessible to both clinicians and the general educated public.

Aner Govrin – Editor

Marion Milner

A Contemporary Introduction

Alberto Stefana and
Alessio Gamba

Routledge
Taylor & Francis Group

LONDON AND NEW YORK

Designed cover image: Michal Heiman, Asylum 1855–2020, The
Sleeper (video, psychoanalytic sofa and Plate 34), exhibition view,
Herzliya Museum of Contemporary Art, 2017.

First published 2024
by Routledge
4 Park Square, Milton Park, Abingdon, Oxon OX14 4RN

and by Routledge
605 Third Avenue, New York, NY 10158

*Routledge is an imprint of the Taylor & Francis Group, an informa
business*

British Library Cataloguing-in-Publication Data
A catalogue record for this book is available from the British
Library

Library of Congress Cataloging-in-Publication Data
A catalog record has been requested for this book

ISBN: 978-1-032-36118-5 (hbk)
ISBN: 978-1-032-36116-1 (pbk)
ISBN: 978-1-003-33033-2 (ebk)

DOI: 10.4324/9781003330332

Typeset in Times New Roman
by Taylor & Francis Books

Contents

Acknowledgments

Stefana, A. (2019). Revisiting Marion Milner's work on creativity and art. *International Journal of Psychoanalysis*, 100(1), 128–147 is reprinted here with permission of Taylor & Francis. Material from this work appears in Chapter 1.

The authors thank Marco De Coppi, Paola Silvia Ferri, and Matteo Terranova for their careful reading and thoughtful comments on Chapters 5 and 6.

Introduction

An outline for the reader

This book is intended both for the normally informed reader of general psychoanalytic theories and for trained psychoanalysts. As far as possible in a psychoanalytic text, we have tried to set out ideas, concepts, and clinical practices in ordinary language. With regard to the content of the text, we will describe Marion Milner's original and substantial contribution to clinical and theoretical psychoanalysis by attempting to follow her professional path, dwelling on a few points of particular interest in terms of her theory of knowledge (which we could perhaps also refer to as 'theory of creativity') and her psychoanalytic practice. In this sense, as we shall see, her talking about creativity is tantamount to outlining a model of health and good psychic adaptation, both on the internal psychological side and on the external environmental side. Similarly, her reflections on being nothing and the ability to stand in the void have value and reach beyond a mere theory of cure or technique. It is her personal point of arrival, within a relentless autobiographical, personal, and introspective quest that is also of value to us, insofar as we can tolerate emptiness, seek the contribution of the other, and explore and explore ourselves toward the unknown within us. From this emptiness, as Blake and Keats pointed out, and before them Heraclitus, can arise that dynamism that brings constant evolution into life.

DOI: 10.4324/9781003330332-1

A brief biography

Marion Blackett Milner (London 1900–98) was one of the main exponents of the Independent Group of the British Psychoanalytical Society, and an inspiration for analysts such as Masud Khan, Wilfred Bion, Francis Tustin, Christopher Bollas, and especially Winnicott—who called her 'one of the big brains of the Society' (Rodman, 1993). However, despite the fact that her main ideas have been deeply absorbed and used by the psychoanalytic mainstream, Milner has always remained on the margins of the latter, probably because she never claimed the 'motherhood' of her ideas, leaving most to believe that they came from famous authors such as Winnicott, Bion, Lacan, and others (Dimitrijević, 2023).

Milner was not only a psychoanalyst: she was first of all a writer and a passionate painter, being an occupational and educational psychologist. "For years," she says, "I had had to decide each weekend, should I shut myself away and paint or should I just live?" (Milner, 1950, p. 156). Her interest in the unconscious was born already at the beginning of her training and professional career until she achieved her psychoanalytic identity. The initial stirrings of interest came from a vague sense of dissatisfaction in her youth. This led her to keep a diary (see Milner, 1934) in which she used to jot down observations on her 'butterfly thoughts,' sensory experiences ('wide attention'), and self-discovery (those aspects of her personality she had previously disavowed: pettiness, fear, vanity, and anger). In this phase (when she used to sign her work under the pseudonym Joanna Field) Milner (1934, 1937, 1987b, 2012) published four diary books, which make up an experimental autobiographical quartet written under the sign of self-analysis (Haughton, 2011; Walters, 2012); "Indeed Milner's diary quartet consists of meta-diaries rather than diaries" (Haughton, 2014, p. 350)—approached the themes of perception, concentration, drawing and art in a completely personal and original way. Her discoveries gradually gave rise to her distinctive way of looking at reality (both internal and external) and also greatly influenced her approach to psychoanalysis.

The subsequent phase was characterized by her interest in and study of the world of work and education. Before deciding to undertake psychoanalytic training, Milner worked as an industrial (organizational) psychologist at the Western Electric Company in Boston

(Massachusetts) and as an investigator at the National Institute of Industrial Psychology headed by Elton Mayo, as well as an educational and research psychologist for the Council of the Girls' Public Day School Trust (Milner, 1938; see also Boyle Spelman, 2023). On the other hand, her cultural interests embraced philosophy, literature, poetry, mythology, religions, spirituality, and, last but not least, figurative art. According to us, it is precisely the meeting and fusion among the breadth of her personal experiences and interests, the rigor and practice of the scientific method acquired through her work as an industrial and educational psychologist, and the realities of the analytic situation which made Milner's approach and contribution unique.

It is the observation of and experiments with problems and blocks in painting and learning that originally led Milner to the idea that awareness of the outside world itself is a creative process, a complex creative interchange between what is inside and what is outside that involves a periodic alternation of fusion and separation.

Through this path characterized by a variety of interests and creative lived experiences, as well as a continuous confrontation with her own inner world but also with different cultural contexts and professions, Milner gradually delved more and more into the psychoanalytic world. She was in fact part of the Imago Group founded by the art historian Adrian Stokes. This was a group of about ten people, in the orbit of Melanie Klein, who met regularly to discuss issues related to art (Bion, Donald Meltzer, and Roger Money-Kyrle, among others, were involved). In addition, she was personally acquainted with the Bloomsbury Group, an influential 'group' of writers, philosophers, intellectuals, and British artists, united in their attribution of importance to the arts (it included figures such as Virginia Woolf and Edward Morgan Forster).

In following Milner's thoughts, there clearly emerges an epistemophilic drive that leads her to constantly question herself and to never be satisfied with her own knowledge. As 'personal' (that is, constructed lacking the contribution of the Other), such knowledge is intrinsically partial because it is. In her writings, the effort to question and confront herself not only with interlocutors outside the circumscribed psychoanalytic world (be they from the worlds of psychology, art, or philosophy), but also with her patients and, before that, with herself, is evident.[1] In doing so, she gradually finds herself understanding intrapsychic and interpersonal dynamics in a different way than initially perceived, with a style of thinking and theoretical work that can be found as much in her descriptions and clinical considerations as in some of her exchanges with her patients. This is all part of an underlying and more general theory and methodology of care and, before that, of psychic functioning, where her experiences and reflections spring from contact with herself and her patients, in a matrix deeply imbued with the empiricism of British culture.

Concerning Milner's psychoanalytic training, it suffices here to recall that she began training at the British Institute of Psychoanalysis in 1940, doing a training analysis with Silvia Payne, after an initial, unsatisfactory Jungian analysis with Irma Putnam in Boston, seen two or three times a week for three months in early 1928. It should be noted here that although in retrospect Milner considered this experience as not really analytical, the resonance with Jungian thought clearly emerges from her writings.[2] Unsatisfied with her first two analytic experiences, in 1943, after becoming a member of the British Psychoanalytical Society, Milner asked Winnicott—her friend, colleague, current supervisor in Susan's case (a girl who lived as a guest in Winnicott's house, who took on the financial burden of treatment), and former analyst of her husband Dennis Milner—to recommend a referral to treat her 'crazy part.' Winnicott offered to be her analyst, and she accepted. For seemingly practical-organizational reasons, the analysis was conducted in Milner's office. After four years, deeply dissatisfied with even this third intricate situation, Milner consulted Clifford Scott, who advised her to interrupt the treatment. Shortly afterward, in 1949, Milner entered analysis with Scott, who had also had Alice Taylor and Claire Britton, Winnicott's first and second wives, in analysis. To complete the general picture of what was Milner's analytic training, let it be recalled that she was supervised by Melanie Klein (much of Milner's analysis with the patient Simon[3]), Joan Riviere, and Ella Freeman Sharpe.[4]

Outline of this book

Using Milner's ideas about the creative process as a base, we will investigate the links between psychoanalysis and unconscious processes in symbol formation and artistic creation (Chapter 1); outline her theorization of the healthy emotional development of the subject (Chapter 2); describe in depth seven concepts within her psychoanalytic thinking (Chapter 3); offer a reading of 'The role of illusion in symbol formation' (Milner, 1952b) to bring to light the importance of imaginative scenarios of both patient and therapist and to make clear some key aspects of her theory and technique (Chapter 4); and extrapolate from the clinical material presented in detail in *The hands of the living God* (Milner, 1969) the underlying theory of technique, whose modifications made by Milner are particularly useful for, but not limited to, the treatment of patients with severe mental issues like psychotic patients (Chapter 5).

Notes

1 In this sense of a tenacious search for 'a life of one's own' (in terms of creativity and personal authenticity), one can read both the description of her having begun an analysis with little awareness of, or perhaps little interest in, the institutional position of her first analyst, Silvia Payne, with respect to 'controversial discussions' (Milner, 1950), as well as her having postponed reading Freud's essay (1929) on 'a case of diabolic possession' (Milner, 1969).

2 It has been noted that Milner appreciated Jung's contribution, especially regarding temperament types, polarities in human life, and mythological orientation (Dragstedt, 1998), as well as his approach to the interpretation of dreams (Malleson, 2023). What she mainly criticized was the limited attention given to the body-dimension (Dragstedt, 1998).

3 This patient was Michael Clyne, nephew of Melanie Klein and son of Erich Klein (named Eric Clyne, from 1937 onwards). In the beginning, this analysis was supervised by Melanie Klein herself (who gave Milner a thorough family background), but the period in which Milner was made into that 'lovely stuff' by the patient, and the period of solemn ritual-like play, were not supervised by her. Owing to a theoretical conflict with Klein- according to Paula Heimann, "Klein was angry with Milner for having produced 'a very original idea' on the capacity for symbol making as the basis of creativity" (Grosskurth, 1987, p. 396)— the patient afterwards went into analysis with Bion.

4 For a very detailed and rich portrait of Marion Milner's life, see the biography by da Emma Letley (2013) and the biographical chapters in *The Marrion Milner Tradition* (Boyle Spelman and Raphael-Leff, 2023).

Chapter 1

The artistic process as a basis for a model of clinical psychoanalytic process

The discovery of 'free drawings'

At the beginning of the 20th century, the artistic and cultural world was animated by theoretical-expressive movements that had irrationality and spontaneous creativity as their center of interest. Among these there was the artistic movement known as Surrealism, born in France around 1920 in an attempt to put some order into the radical disorder of Dadaism. In continuation from the latter, Surrealism foregrounded the importance the exaltation of non-sense and irrationality, the wide use of mechanisms of the unconscious (psychic automatism) and of randomness. The sur-reality resides in attributing to dream work the same quality of presence, solidity, and definiteness typically attributed to external reality.

The definition of the surrealist movement is provided in the *Manifestes du Surréalisme*, where we read:

> Psychic automatism in its pure state, is the proposal to express—verbally, and by means of the written word, or in any other manner—the actual functioning of thought. It is dictated by thought, in the absence of any control exercised by reason, exempt from any aesthetic or moral concern.
>
> (...) Surrealism is based on the belief in a superior reality of certain forms of previously neglected associations, in the omnipotence of dream, in the disinterested play of thought. It tends to ruin once and for all, all other psychic mechanisms and to be a substitute itself for them in solving all the principal problems of life.
>
> (Breton, 1924, p. 26)

DOI: 10.4324/9781003330332-2

The connection with Freud's *The Interpretation of Dreams* (1899) is noticeable here, to such an extent that, according to René Magritte (1938), "Surrealism demands for our waking life a freedom comparable to the one we enjoy when we dream."[1]

Milner knew the surrealist movement; we know that between January and February 1939 she visited the joint exhibition of Reuben Mednikoff and Grace Pailthorpe (also a psychoanalyst) at the Guggenheim Jeune Gallery in London, who made extensive use of automatic drawing (Maclagan, 1992). The idea behind Pailthorpe's work was that "there must be somewhere a quicker way to the deeper layers of the unconscious than by the long drawn-out couch method, and I had a feeling that it was through art" (Pailthorpe; cited in Stefana and Montanaro, 2023, p. 4). Pailthorpe, with Mednikoff's collaboration, conceived what she named the satiation-analysis technique, in which the analyst gave the patient drink and food before the analytic session to relieve any anxiety and then encourages him or her "to be as free as possible and to avoid, if he or she can, a desire to alter shapes that first appear (…) to paint without caring about results (…) to be loose and free with the paint" (Pailthorpe; cited in Montanaro and Stefana, 2024). The analyst could not help the patient while painting but could make gestures of approval, permission, sympathy, and reassurance, if the patient showed any sign of needing it. Both analyst and patient had to write notes on any thoughts and feelings they had, and every production was followed by detailed explanations.

The previous year (1938), tired of her own drawings that seemed more like accurate copies of external reality, and in conjunction with the initiation of her personal analysis (which a year later became part of a process of psychoanalytic training), Milner began her study on how to learn to draw. This research and subsequent reflections upon her drawings, she eventually used as a kind of internal dialogue, even in the analysis with Sylvia Payne (Sayers, 2002). Milner believed it might be interesting to try to draw something without any conscious intention[2] and was shocked to discover, almost by chance, that sometimes it is possible to execute sketches or drawings, allowing eye and hand to be free to do exactly what they wished, without the conscious seeking of a preordained result, without the inclination to draw 'something.'[3] Milner thus began to look at drawings in the way Freud approached dreams, and she realized that in implementing this 'free' method, as she termed it, moods and ideas, represented by the signs of the pencil on paper, could emerge, and that these, on a conscious level, seemed totally absent.

Therefore, free drawings were permeated by the shape of emotions and pure thoughts (conscious and unconscious) of the one who produced them. This conformed to what the psychoanalyst Herbert Silberer (1909) described as a 'functional phenomenon,' that is, the phenomenon by which, in the dream images, the emotional state of the dreamer is represented, not the content of thought. As a result, a drawing can turn out to be interesting only if it represents a mix of the external world and aspects of the artist's self, and this is expressed by the unique signs the artist leaves on a sheet of paper expressing his inner processes. It is here interesting to note that Milner's thought was certainly deeply influenced by Carl Gustav Jung's concept of the 'art as active imagination,' as well as by that of 'image.' Jung talked about the transcendent function of art, which is the bridge between conscious and unconscious, to describe how:

> often it is necessary to clarify a vague content by giving it visible form. This can be done by drawing, painting or modelling. Often the hands know how to solve a riddle with which the intellect has wrestled in vain. By shaping it, one goes on dreaming the dream in greater detail in the waking state, and the initially incomprehensible, isolated event is integrated into the sphere of the total personality, even though it remains at first unconscious to the subject.
>
> (Jung, 1916, p. 180)

Regarding the concept of 'image,' Jung defined it as:

> a condensed expression of the psychic situation as a whole (…), an expression of the unconscious as well as the conscious situation of the moment. The interpretation of its meaning, therefore, can start neither from the conscious

alone nor from the unconscious alone, but only from their reciprocal relationship.

(Jung, 1921, pp. 613–614)

It should also be noted that oftentimes Milner used the word image interchangeably with the word symbol.

One must also bear in mind that by the mid-nineteenth century, with the studies on *Einfühlung* (empathy) by Friedrich Theodor Vischer and his son Robert, together with the later contributions of key thinkers such as Theodor Lipps and Aby Warburg, a certain emphasis began to be put on phenomena such as the tactile values of a work of art, the bodily responses that can be elicited in the viewer and, more generally, the importance of empathy in the viewer's aesthetic experience of an artwork. According to these theorists, it is the identification with the artistic work, similarly to what you can experience with another person, that makes it possible to experience beauty and its modifications, such as the ugly and the sublime. The artwork is therefore considered no longer as a mere object (in a non-psychoanalytic sense) but as an expressive structure (Pinotti, 2010), in which an inside shows itself in an outside, a character in a gesture, a soul in a body.

It became clear to Milner (1950) that painting is also deeply connected to the problems of distance and separation between subject and object, and she realized that the edges of objects in the reality of nature are not so fixed, clear, and compact as 'reasonable' and reassuring common sense would want: "When really looked at in relation to each other their outlines were not clear and compact, as I had always supposed them to be, they continually become lost in shadow" (p. 18). We may affirm that the reading of Harold Speed's *The Practice and Science of Drawing* helped Milner to visualize the objects that surrounded her in a new way. We cite the following passage to that effect:

Most of the earliest forms of drawing known to us in history (...) are largely in the nature of outline drawings. This is a remarkable fact considering the somewhat remote relation lines have to the complete phenomena of vision. Outlines can only be said to exist in appearances as the boundaries of masses. But even here a line seems a poor thing from the visual point of view; as the boundaries are not always clearly defined, but are continually merging into the surrounding mass and losing themselves to be caught up again later on and defined once more.

(Speed, 1913, p. 50)

In fact, it was at one time Leonardo da Vinci who used the technique of *sfumato*, consisting of the smooth transition from one colour tone to another, blending the colours into each other instead of putting them side by side for a contrasting effect. From his scientific studies, Leonardo had come to believe that no form in nature ever occurs fixed, so in his paintings the edges of the objects portrayed vanish, and the plastic relief of the images thus become attenuated. The English painter and father of romantic landscape as well as precursor to Impressionism, Joseph Mallord William Turner, also made an important contribution to this discourse on contours in painting. Indeed, owing to the particular use Turner makes of light and colour, the lines marking the boundaries of the objects, in his paintings, become obliterated. Shapes seem to lose their sense of definiteness and material quality because those very lines which should circumscribe the various figures and separate them from the background have been eliminated. We must also note the important contributions of the Post-Impressionists, such as Paul Cézanne and Vincent van Gogh. Such a list of artists may appear—and from the perspective of an art historian it indeed is—a naïve grouping of painters belonging to different centuries and different artistic movements; however, the common thread that binds them together is Milner's knowledge of their paintings (see for example 1950, 1987b).

The book entitled *On Not Being Able to Paint* (1950) was the result of numerous creative experiments made by Milner starting from September 1939 which were inspired to some extent by her seeing the paintings of the above-mentioned artists. Milner conducted an analysis of the content of her drawings and of her own mental processes that accompanied these creative experiences. The work turned out to be "an attempt to discover, within the confines of a specific field, something about the nature of the forces [supplementary] that bring order out of chaos" (Milner, 1957, p. 216), and at the same time, an attempt to reveal something about the inner workings of psychic creativity.

Through these reflections on boundaries and the dialectic between chaos and order, Milner comes to see the certainty of the existence of borders as a defence against the fear of being crazy, "fear of losing all sense of separating boundaries; particularly the boundaries between the tangible realities of the external world and the imaginative realities of the inner world of feeling and idea" (p. 19). In other words, what some people call 'going crazy' is, at least partly, their way of experiencing and describing the lessening of their own inner rigid organization (i.e., strict boundaries between subjects, emotions of opposing valence, etc.)—which in fact needs to happen before they could find a healthy one. Some of these people have some awareness of a 'force' in them that has to do with the growth of the true Self, and that drove them to break down false inner organizations that do not really belong to them. It is:

> something which can also be deeply feared, as a kind of creative fury that will not let them rest content with a merely compliant adaptation; and also feared because of the temporary chaos it must cause when the integrations on a false basis are in the process of being broken down in order that a better one may emerge.
>
> (Milner, 1969, p. 431)

The process of symbolization

With the writing of *On not Being Able to Paint*, Milner became more and more aware of not being able to precisely define 'psychic creativity.' Only later did she manage to define it as the ability to form a symbol for the emotions[4] in art and for knowledge in science. This meaning is in keeping with the ideas of the scholar of aesthetics, Susanne K. Langer (1942, 1953), who considers art as the creation of symbolic forms representing an expression of the artist's own conception of his/her feelings. For Langer the artist does not express his feelings directly, but he articulates them through forms of organization—those symbolic forms of which, the artist avails him/herself, during the act of creation, in order to convey the emotion that the self-same symbolic forms embody.

There are also traceable points of contact with the thinking of the poet William Wordsworth (1800), mentioned by Milner (1950) herself. He claimed that:

> Poetry (…) takes its origin from emotion recollected in tranquillity: the emotion is contemplated by a species of reaction where tranquillity gradually disappears, and an emotion, similar to that which was before the subject of contemplation is gradually produced, and does itself actually exist in the mind. In this mood a successful composition generally begins, and in a mood similar to this it is carried on.

(p. 183)

According to Milner (1952b), symbol formation is preceded by an identification of a primary with a secondary object, whereby the latter is different from the former in reality, though they are equivalent from an affective point of view (of course this affective equivalence does not mean that the subject actually confuses them). For clarity, it should be noted that by primary object we mean the object, or that part of it, to which the child initially relates. It is in this primary object that the subject tries to find a representation of his moods, the acquisition of which would remove the need to abandon these feelings. The secondary object is another piece of the world (a person, a work of art, etc.) that becomes significant as a result of the process of symbolization.

There are two concepts to which Milner refers when reflecting on this process of fusion: fantasy, because only in internal reality can two separate items merge into one, and illusion (which refers to potential space as described by Winnicott, 1951), implying a fantastic relationship with an object perceived externally. Milner (1950, 1952b[5]) understands illusion as a necessary tool for a healthy adaptation to reality, and not at all as a failure in the adaptive process. Indeed, she argued—following the thought of the American philosopher George Santayana (1920)—that the existence of boundaries between 'me' and 'not-me' is not known innately, but it is something which is experienced even though one might not be aware of it. The acquisition of this knowledge is in fact a slow and painstaking process for the baby: "our inner dream and outer perception both spring from a common source or primary phase of experience in which the two are not distinguished, a primary 'madness' which all of us have lived through and to which at times we can return (Milner, 1950, p. 33). Thus Milner grounds her notion of illusion in the sensorial experience of fusion between self and object. As the mother steadily becomes less attuned to the needs of the baby, the development of transitional phenomena and potential space will take place, and it is in this context that mental space, alongside the space for playing and symbolizing, is created. Here we have a modification to the Freudian hypothesis: Freud implies the necessity of overcoming illusion, whereas Milner the necessity of maintaining a degree of illusion.

In both his artistic and clinical work, Milner brings to the fore this multiplicity of gazes and how it inevitably intertwines with reality, with what is perceived as subjective and what is perceived as objective, with what is considered healthy (creative, personal) or pathological, and with the perception of the boundaries of a s/object. Furthermore, as will be better seen later, Milner leads us to reflect on the various ways and stages in which the primary object stretches to the secondary object.

In a certain sense, although not quite in Milner's words, one can also consider the concept of 'madness'—something we periodically return to in order to access creativity—in a different and less conventional way: an egosyntonic aspect that is part of the constellation of personality. Consequently, daily life is enriched with a 'nuance' that it would be reductive to place only within a psychological or psychiatric nosography. Milner implicitly suggests that the perception or conceptualization of what is objective/external *versus* subjective/internal requires a much broader but perhaps also simpler open-mindedness. Suffice it to think here of how, for example, the way one views a lover is a condensation of perceptions, thoughts, and affections born in the personal psyche-soma of the observer, thus something not at all different from an artistic creation.

The imaginative concentration

Beginning in the 1930s, Milner began to think about Zen Buddhism and the mystical traditions of both the East and the West in an attempt to learn more about methods to produce changes in consciousness by means of concentrating on the inner awareness of the body. In this way, she came to support the need for a particular type of imaginative focus (active and immobile at the same time), a contemplative action that enriches the outside world of certain qualities matching the subject's own (Milner, 1956a, 1956b). Such a state of deep concentration is a sensory experience in which you find an empty space,[6] a 'uterine space' from which something new can be born. The culminating point of such a process of imaginative illusion is the ecstasy, i.e., the emotional experience of searching and finding a substitute, the familiar in the unfamiliar (the reference here is to Wordsworth, 1800, according to whom the pleasure that comes from perceiving the similar in the dissimilar is essential for maintaining mental activity). The term ecstasy, in other words, expresses a feeling that asserts the subjective rightness of what one is realizing (for example, an artistic work) (Featherstone, 2023), the delight inherent in identification and recognition that extend the emotional and cognitive cognition of the outer world (Scott, 2023). Being in such a state of ecstasy is like being in touch with one's own overwhelming ability to create the world. In this sense we can remember the famous 'Art creates Nature' statement:[7]

> By suffusing, through giving it form, the not-me objective material with the me – subjective psychic content, it makes the not–me 'real,' realizable. (…) So what the artist (…) is doing, fundamentally, is not recreating in the sense of making again what has been lost (although he is doing this), but creating what is, because he is creating the power to perceive it. By continually breaking up the established familiar patterns (familiar in his particular culture and time in history) of

logical common-sense divisions of me–not–me, he really is creating 'nature,' including human nature. And he does this by unmasking old symbols and making new ones, thus incidentally making it possible for us to see that the old symbol was a symbol; whereas before we thought the symbol was in 'reality' because we had nothing else to compare it with[8]. In this sense he is continually destroying 'nature' and re-creating nature—which is perhaps why the depressive anxieties can so easily both inhibit and be relieved by successful creative work in the arts.

(Milner, 1957, pp. 228–229)

What Milner tells us is that the poetic genius[9] hidden in all of us, the one that 'creates' the outside world, discovering something familiar in what is unknown, needs a particular kind of imaginative concentration, a contemplative widespread attention that enriches what one recognizes as a particular quality of one's self. This concentration within the self and within the body is not to be seen exclusively as a regressive movement, but also, if not more, as a pre-logical subject-object fusion, as well as a body-mind fusion (Milner, 1960, 1969). Concerning the 'poetic genius' belonging to every individual, it is interesting that even the philosopher Jacques Maritain (1953) believed that every person is potentially capable of having 'poetic intuition' (he places it at the root of the creative process). Ronald Britton (2015) helps us to fully understand this suggesting that "poetic revelation is psychic reality," and that therefore "psychic reality is the only reality" (pp. 119–120). The creative person is thus the one who permits himself this ability, even at the cost of experiencing the pain of being in contact with that specific wound, which, however, is also a source of creativity.

The experience of the artist

At this point it should be understood that the core around which Milner's study on creativity and art has revolved is the personal affective experience of the artist at work. An essential part of this experience is contained within the artist's body. The psychophysical rhythm of a person immersed in creating a work of art, whatever it may be, is unique and unrepeatable. It is the source of life that animates true works of art, those creations that are an externalization, through lines and colours (in the case of the painting), of the uniqueness of the artist's own psychophysical structure (Remember that in 1935, Sharpe, after a careful study of the qualities that distinguish the artist, had identified the rhythmic movement of the body of the artist who is creating as the source of the beauty of the work).

Milner (1957) tells us that the psychophysical organism of everyone has an intrinsic rhythmic potential that can acquire a more stable order with respect to the belief in an either externally or internally imposed order (the conscious planning mind).

More generally we can say that:

> what the painter does conceptualize in non-verbal symbols is the astounding experiences of how it feels to be alive, the experiences known from inside, of being a moving, living body in space, with capacities to relate oneself to other objects in space. And included in this experience of being alive is the very experiencing of the creative process itself.
>
> (Milner, 1957, p. 227)

In this regard, Milner argues that the achievement of balance and stability found its roots in the relationship of reciprocity that has been experienced between the bodily rhythms of the subject and the person who so dedicatedly and lovingly cares for this body. Consider a child who, in his imaginative scenario, creates his mother. Of course, we know that it is not like this, but he will dedicate himself entirely to this illusion, at least while he is building it, that is, while he is in a state of ecstasy because of the subjective reality of what he is creating: it is the situation in which the mother "places the actual breast just there where the infant is ready to create, and at the right moment" (Winnicott, 1953, p. 95). Furthermore, it is equally important that there be a possibility of reciprocal exchange between the individual qualities of the chosen medium of expression (see Rayner, 1991)—which in this example is the mother (or the analyst, in a different context)—and the psychophysical rhythm of the baby (or the patient). It is the mother herself who constitutes the expressive means, the pliable medium (a concept to which we shall return later) necessary for creativity to have a way to express itself.

The bodily experience, more specifically those interests invested in the various stages of psychosexual development (the oral, anal, and phallic stages), plays a key role in generating those symbols that everyone uses in the creative process. This is what is meant when we say that metaphors originate in the body.

Some considerations of aesthetic experience within artistic creation

A key element in psychic creativity or more specifically in the formulation of a symbol is the necessity of finding the familiar in the unfamiliar, with similar results, as recalled by Jones. Fulfilling this requirement allows the author of the symbol to overcome natural fears (the unknown being inherently disturbing), gain knowledge of the reality of detachment and separation, with all of the accompanying anxiety, and establish object relations. This process is made possible by "the basic identifications which (...) require an ability to tolerate a temporary loss of sense of self, a temporary giving up of the discriminating ego which stands apart and tries to see things objectively and rationally and without emotional colouring" (Milner, 1952b, p. 189). The mental state of the subject immersed in this process is what the art historian Bernard Berenson (1948) describes as 'aesthetic moment:'

> In visual art the aesthetic moment is that fleeting instant, so brief as to be almost timeless, when the spectator is at one with the work of art he is looking at, or with actuality of any kind that the spectator himself sees in terms of art, as form and colour. He ceases to be his ordinary self, and the picture or building, statue, landscape, or aesthetic actuality is no longer outside himself. The two become one entity; time and space are abolished and the spectator is possessed by one awareness. When he recovers workaday consciousness it is as if he had been initiated into illuminating, formative mysteries. In short, the aesthetic moment is a moment of mystic vision.
>
> (pp. 84–85)

This mental state of deep and harmonious interaction between internal and external, me and not-me, subject and object, in which the variations in the perception of existence or non-existence of the boundary of one's body play a key role, involves the feeling of enclosing the whole world (both good and bad objects) inside one's own body (Milner, 1950, 1952b). Such a feeling corresponds to the 'oceanic' one described by Romain Rolland (1927, quoted in Freud, 1929) as "an indissoluble bond, of being one with the external world as a whole" (p. 65), "of limitlessness and of a bond with the universe" (p. 68) which Milner (1969) called "a sea of undifferentiated being" (p. 29).

It is during this 'aesthetic moment' that the viewer of the work of art identifies with it and dissolves completely into it. It is clear that the anxiety that the subject feels in these moments of immersion into creative depths is an integral part of the creative process, therefore it should not be avoided or denied. On a perceptual level, the subject must be able to arouse a contemplative, extensive attention, implying a kind of deconstruction of the mind's conditioning, which opens up the possibility of having a more complete experience of both one's own self and the external world, to 'actively' abandon oneself to the moment.

According to Milner (1956a), the creative process, resulting in a cancellation of the separation between subject and object (a separation upon which logical thinking is based), takes place within the context of the empty gaps in our mental activity on the surface: "it must be clear to anyone who looks inward that our mental life does progress with a movement rather like a porpoise" (p. 195), where there is a cyclical sequence of immerging and re-emerging with respect to the surface of the water, or more precisely the border between the conscious and the unconscious. Milner (1957) considers:

> the logical terms in which the capacity for symbol formation is thought about are perhaps less important than the pre-logical. I want to suggest that it is the terms in which we think, on the deeper non-verbal levels of the psyche, about this specifically human capacity for making symbols that in part determines the way the capacity works in us.
>
> (p. 217)

Here, too, we can trace a meeting of minds with Langer (1942), whose work was appreciated by Milner (see for example 1950, 1952b, 1956a), who differentiates the verbal discursive thought processes from the non-verbal and non-discursive ones (whose rules, as Langer highlights, were initially formulated by Freud). But to be more accurate, one can see the substantial influence that Jacques Maritain and Anton Ehrenzweig have on Milner's view of the creative process, who has frequently acknowledged her debt towards them (see for example 1950, 1952b, 1956a). Maritain (1953) believed that modern painters are more focused upon the painting itself—or better, on the particular, psychological process in which that they are fully engaged as they create the *objet d'art*— rather than being goal-directed (i.e., representing something); this doesn't mean that the art object is not important, but that being driven by a relentless search for a deeper reality, the artist necessarily goes beyond the appearance of things. The driving force of this process resides in the impossibility of the artist's creative subjectivity reaching the conscious level unless in communion with what is outside of the self. For the French philosopher, at the moment of creation, the self and 'things' are simultaneously grasped, because here the splitting between subject-object, typical of logical thinking, has ceased. Ehrenzweig (1953) speaks of a tendency towards articulation on the part of surface mental activity (logical-rational thought), and he also speaks of deep mental activity (unconscious pre-logical thought), whose working manner seems chaotic to the surface mind, but in actuality is able to understand a greater number of things than the surface mind. Moreover, Ehrenzweig points out that Freud, William James and the *Gestalt* psychologists were among those that had indicated this tendency towards articulation on the part of surface mental activity.[10]

Focusing further on the concept of creativity according to Milner (1956a), it is possible to assert that creativity cannot simply be attributed to the mental state, defined as 'oceanic feeling'—the feeling of being one with the universe—, but it is strictly tied to the continuous oscillating between the state in which the Self of the child (and then of the artist or of an adult) is not yet differentiated from the surrounding external world, and the state characterized by the surface mind activity, in which things and the self are grasped separately[11]. Such cyclical alternating is in part passively experienced, but it is also sought actively with the intention of producing something, remembering that the primary function of art is not the recovery of lost objects, but the 'creation' of new ones. But for it to take place within the subject, a situation is needed that makes it possible to surrender to *rêverie* and to the illusion of oneness, a context that is offered by painting, both to the artist as well as the viewer (Milner, 1957). Therefore what needs to be reached or recovered is a mental state (with respect to the material, the subject/object, or the work of art), resembling that of childhood's dual union, where the self and the not-self are not very distinct, because only in these mental states is it possible to experience creativity (Spitz, 1985). Christopher Bollas (1987) mirrors this position when he conceptualizes the first human aesthetic experience within the idiom of formal aesthetic experience—understood, in this instance, as the way in which the child experiences the idiom of his mother's care. However, the attempt of some authors to ground creativity and aesthetic experience on the mother-child encounter raises an important question: what about the exquisitely original artists who had little, or no good-enough maternal care?[12] Probably, as Gregorio Kohon (2016) points out:

> it may be something more mysterious and complex than [the vicissitudes of the encounter with the primary object]. (…) It is conceivable that the existential memory present in aesthetic *jouissance* takes place in the context of experiences other than that mythical primary encounter. Its significance may have started somewhere else, in a psychic place other than with the mother, and progressively moved back and forth along different paths.
>
> (p. 4)

Furthermore, outside of a psychoanalytic clinical context, wondering why aesthetic experiences exist, rather than how they operate, is perhaps of minor importance (Maclagan, 2001).

Taking Otto Rank's (1932) work based on art and artists as her starting-point, Milner (1952b, 1956a) opted to characterize art as a bridge between inner reality and outer reality, where the boundaries merge and not without getting a bit confused.

Therefore, art is a method that allows the adult to escape the mortal sterility inherent in a fixed and exclusively 'objective' perception of the world. This can occur because art makes the illusion of unity and a pre-logic fusion between subject and object possible, allowing a relationship of reciprocity between internal and external realities. In other words, art generates that necessary illusion in order to initiate a creative rapport with reality. Crucial to this process is the role of the surrounding framework. Its goal is to guarantee that all that is represented within it is not an objective reality but an illusion; in this sense what we perceive inside the frame has to be interpreted symbolically, as a metaphor (a way of knowing and communicating), expressive of the psychic reality (Milner, 1952a). At the same time, in terms of what was said about the necessity of an oscillation between the illusion of unity and the absence of illusion, Stokes (1955) claims that it is by means of the double experience of: a state of fusion between the artist and the material chosen in advance, something at once totally separate and connected, and of a state of separateness that the chaotic material can draw on in order to adopt an aesthetic form. It is curios to note that here Milner did not differ from classical psychoanalysis in its insistence on dualistic thinking, or rather that there are two discrete ways of thinking and seeing one peculiar of infancy and one of adulthood. The originality of Winnicott's conception of the transitional object actually lies in the overcoming of this "polarization of distinction and merger" (Eigen, 1983, p. 424)—"into transitional space where one-ness and two-ness can coexist and one can inhabit *both* inner- and outer-world reality" (Marks, 2014, p. 95).

It is obvious that, through the use of an expressive *medium*, artistic activity allows one to experience the act of creating an object. (If one's emotional development during childhood went reasonably well this is actually a re-experience). Milner (1952b, 1956a) tells us that the expressive medium, being flexible, submits to what is done to it without imposing any constraints. It allows itself to take the form of one's own fantasies, or according to Christopher Caudwell (1937), the artist uses his chosen medium of expression like a poet uses words. But the expressive medium is also something which, in all likelihood, the artist tends to idealize to a great extent. Only if the artist loves this medium to the extent that he can become sensitive to its real qualities and potential (and therefore take full advantage of the pliability of the material) will the object created live up to the idealization. After all, art and expression exist only where material is used as a means (Dewey, 1934). It seems that artists can only be ambivalent towards their medium; they love and hate it and fight it constantly.

The creation of something new, and not the original subconscious wish symbolized by the object created, is the most important aspect of every work of creativity (a new piece of the external world that through the process of symbolization has satisfied the primary need for unity, shifting interest onto the real object). The artist moulds his own private experiences into a new form that can be incorporated into the social world of art, creating symbols that let the inner life leak through. In this way the artist reduces, without completely removing, the gap between experience itself and the linguistic and perceivable means of expressing emotions and cognitions of the inner world. If it be true that real art is, at first, a matter of feelings (Kandinsky, 1914), then the work of art, via the 'form' through which it has become visible, represents the vehicle of communication for the emotions and cognitions of the artist. This means that the symbols already discovered by the artist acquire full meaning (for him/her) (Milner, 1952b). It is worthy of note that, according to the historian Erwin Panofsky (1955), the 'form' impressed on the artistic creation is one of those three elements (the other two are the idea [or the subject] and the content) that all come together in the aesthetic experience.

What Milner (1956a) wants us to understand is that:

the unconscious mind, by the very fact of its not clinging to the distinction between self and other, seer and seen, can do things that the conscious logical mind cannot do. By being more sensitive to the samenesses rather than the differences between things, by being passionately concerned with finding 'the familiar in the unfamiliar' (…), it does just what Maritain says it does; it brings back blood to the spirit, passion to intuition. It provides the source for all renewal and rebirth,

mutual exchange between the analyst and the patient, enabling them to enter into a dialogue about the patient's deeply unconscious issues. It must be remembered that Milner (see 1969) also resorted to the method of free drawing within her psychotherapy work itself, encouraging her patients to use this type of drawing as a means to communicate those feelings for which they had no words. These are methods that facilitate therapeutic work by creating "a context in which the absence of conscious intentions will allow feelings to emerge" (Mitchell, 2000, p. 131).

3 It is worth mentioning here another passage of the *Manifestes du Surréalisme*: "After you have settled yourself in a place as favourable as possible to the concentration of your mind upon itself, have writing materials brought to you. Put yourself in as passive, or receptive, a state of mind as you can. Forget about your genius, your talents, and the talents of everyone else. Keep reminding yourself that literature is one of the saddest roads that leads to everything. Write quickly, without any preconceived subject, fast enough so that you will not remember what you're writing and be tempted to reread what you have written. The first sentence will come spontaneously, so compelling is the truth that with every passing second there is a sentence unknown to our consciousness which is only crying out to be heard" (Breton, 1924, pp. 29–30).

4 The concept of artistic creation as the representation or symbol of emotions appears to be today an extreme simplification. Presently, artistic creation is conceived, rather less poetically, but surely less naïvely, as the consequence of the united and coordinated action of cognitive processes (perception, thought, imagination, attention, memory etc.), of affective processes (see Argenton, 1996; Tan, 2000), as well as somatic ones. In addition, the idea of the work of art as a representation of the artist's emotions that have created it, is extremely limited; it has to be amplified to the point of including the internal world of the artist, his/her way of 'seeing' and 'understanding' reality and existence (Bartoli, 2003).

5 It is worth remembering that "Aspects of symbolism in comprehension of the not-self" was written between 1950 and 1951 (see Milner, 1969, p. 249), that is, before Winnicott read his paper "Transitional objects and transitional phenomena" at the British Psycho-Analytical Society, on 30 May 1951. Milner anticipates some aspects of Winnicott's transitional phenomenon concept showing that if the patient finds that the therapist (or better still, his/her mind) is not acquiescent (that is not capable of taking the form of the patient's fantasy), but his toys are, he thus finds an escape route from the act of hitting the therapist, which causes anxiety, because neither of them should surrender. The child's experience in this case is just like the experience of a person

who, for instance, while drawing, concentrates on what the lines sketched on the paper can mean for him/her (Milner, 1950).

6 It is worth keeping in mind that such a void, linked to the abandonment of reassuring logical thought, is potentially also a space where anxiety and terror can lead to an irreversible depression. In order to bear the horror of such an empty space, Milner affirms the need to be able to accept doubt and uncertainty. Already in 1943 she speaks about this, hinting at the 'Negative Capability' that the romantic poet John Keats writes about in a letter to his brothers on December 21, 1817: "when a man is capable of being in uncertainties, mysteries, doubts, without any irritable reaching after fact and reason" (Keats, 1895, p. 57). For a discussion about Bion's O and Milner's zero (pregnant emptiness) see Michael Eigen (2015, 2023).

7 Oscar Wilde famously cited art as the source of nature (Johnston, 2016).

8 The poet and art historian Herbert E. Read (1951) highlights the need to distinguish two very different meanings attributed to the word symbol: one possesses a sense of the mingling together of two tangible objects, or a tangible object with an immaterial idea; the other a sense of losing that initial separation thus making the symbol a form of original expression. Concerning this second way of interpreting the word symbol, Segal (1950) speaks of 'symbolic equation:' the symbol is confused with that which is symbolized; there is no distinction between the two (a famous example is the one of the violinist who when asked by the doctor why he stopped playing since he got sick, answered that he had no intention of masturbating in public).

9 The poet, painter, and engraver William Blake (1788) writes "That the Poetic Genius is the true Man, and that the body or outward form of Man is derived from the Poetic Genius. Likewise that the forms of all things are derived from their Genius, which by the Ancients was call'd an Angel & Spirit & Demon."

10 The *Gestalt* psychologists had also examined the problem of the ambiguity of objects, specifically the problem of ambiguity and the non-definition of the object in relation to its context. Pictorial perception was also part of this branch of study.

11 Ernst Kris (1952), an exponent of Ego Psychology, talks about the creative process in terms of a controlled regression of the ego to the primary process, where the ego, partially reducing the control of its superior functions, maintains a certain autonomy with respect to the id.

12 Possibly, at least for some of these people, it is the creative use of the fusion between the Self and the bad primary object. This hypothesis finds support in the fact that even ugly things (Eco, 2004, 2007) or disturbing and disagreeable experiences (Tomlin, 2008) create an aesthetic experience. Thus, similarly to the good object, the bad primary object can elicit an aesthetic experience once it transcends its pragmatic value.

Chapter 2

Emotional development of the subject

The passage from the primary to the secondary object

To better understand Milner's contribution to clinical psycho-analysis, it is helpful to know her theorization of the healthy emotional-psychological development of the subject. In fact, the importance of early development, which includes the feelings that the parents have in regard to the child, is central in Milner's (1945, 1952b) work with children, but is also an integral part of her work with adolescents and adults (Milner, 1969), as one must constantly return during their clinical work to what has transpired throughout the years, following the earliest developmental stages. Furthermore, it has been suggested that an implicit equation between baby-caregiver and patient-therapist drives each psychoanalytic model and technique (Raphael-Leff, 2023).

While being aware that Milner's conception of internal psychic reality is largely influenced by Melanie Klein (1948), it must be emphasized that there is a substantial difference when comparing the two analysts' work. This difference lies in the greater importance that Milner assigns to the actual influence of the environment on the process guiding the child into understanding what to perceive as good and what to experience as persecutory. For Milner (1952b), the identification or fusion of a primary object—i.e., the object, or that part of it, to which the child initially relates—with a secondary one, which according to her while different objects are dynamically identical from an emotional point of view, is the precursor to symbol formation. According to the British Object Relations School, it is in the 'primary object' (Jones, 1916; Klein, 1923, 1930; Milner, 1952b) that the subject tries to find a representation

DOI: 10.4324/9781003330332-3

of their moods, and it is the acquisition of this primary object which relieves the child of the need to abandon these feelings. It is in this primary object that the subject tries to find a representation of his moods, the acquisition of which would remove the need to abandon these feelings. The secondary object is another piece of the world—a person, a work of art, an institution, etc.—that becomes significant as a result of the process of symbolization.

But what is it that brings the infant or child to shift their interest from the primary to the secondary object? According to Klein (1923, 1930), the subject passes from the primary to the secondary object, owing either to the actual loss of the object or alternatively owing to the existence of an internal conflict, forcing the child to transfer their attention to and invest in another object, in order to protect the primary object from their aggression, and protect themselves from feelings of guilt. Milner (1952b) agreed with Klein's statement, that symbolization is the basis of all talents and skills, and precisely those skills that allow a connection with the surrounding world. She argued that premature ego development inhibits the capacity for symbol formation (*ibid.*), but did not accept the idea of *inborn* envy, which was central to Klein (1957; see also Hinshelwood, 1989)—indeed it was precisely because of this important difference of opinion that Milner stopped attending Klein's seminars for analysts, after 1954 (Milner, 1987a). In contrast to Klein, Milner (1952b) believed that envy was linked to premature ego formation, owing to a childhood in which primary omnipotence had not had enough space to develop (see also Winnicott, 1962). Having noted the infant's need for the establishment of object relations, Milner deviated from the Kleinian view, which she saw as having a limited focus on the need for reparation. Instead she integrated a Kleinian view with the model outlined by Ernest Jones (1916), who identified the need to endow the external world with aspects of the self that make it familiar as the basis of the process of identification (Jones, 1916). The projection of the self onto the world, of which Jones wrote, was inspired by an essay by Sándor Ferenczi (1913), describing the ways the child tries to experience and filter external reality, therein discovering his or her own organs and their functions. It is notable that Ferenczi's essay provides the basis of what Klein (1946) would later call projective identification, or at least one aspect of it. Following a line of thought similar to that of Ella F. Sharpe (1935), Milner distanced herself from the Kleinian framework, as she did not see this process as an 'obstacle to progress'—an expression of the desire for comfort and pleasure, contrasting with the demands of daily life—, but as the only possible way for the infant to begin to understand the world (Milner, 1952b, pp. 181–182).

Winnicott (1951) wrote: "the mother places the actual breast just there where the infant is ready to create, and at the right moment" (p. 95). Mother and child, nipple and tongue, co-operate to produce and reinforce the illusion of continuity; these illusory states of oneness are considered a necessary phase in the achievement of the experience of twoness.

Milner, influenced by the thought of the American philosopher George Santayana (1920), explored the existence of the 'me–not-me' boundaries, not as innate knowledge, but as something slowly and arduously discovered by the child: "our inner dream and outer perception both spring from a common source or primary phase of experience in which the two are not distinguished, a primary 'madness' which all of us have lived through and to which at times we can return" (Milner, 1950, p. 33).

In parentheses, we would like to point out here that current knowledge based on infant research (for example Beebe et al., 2016, 2021; Stern, 1985) and infant observation (for example Reid, 1997; Vallino and Macciò, 2004) tells us that research into a primary narcissism (interpreted as primary autism), or self-other undifferentiation in the newborn, has not brought results that would support such hypotheses; what has, on the other hand, been observed is the newborn's capacity to execute mental processes of the perceptive and mnemonic sort, including those that allow one to distinguish between the internal and external, the me and the not-me. Here, it is interesting to note that a study on contingent communication between parents and preterm infants in the neonatal intensive care unit showed the presence of sequential bidirectional patterns of communication between caregiver and preterm infants at 35 weeks postmenstrual age (Lavelli et al., 2022; Stefana et al., 2020).

However, this may not be valid for the neo-natal unconscious mind, the proto-mental, as theorized by the Italian psychoanalyst Antonio Imbasciati (2006). Starting from an empirical point of view, Imbasciati arrives at the conclusion that if the neonate "is unable to distinguish an 'inside' from an 'outside'—a 'me' from a 'not me'—he will be unable to organize those visual differences effectively," because "the set of stimuli from the objects and receptors does not meet with an apparatus equipped to discern any organization in them" (p. 76). "It can therefore be argued that a neonate does not perceive (in the strict sense of the word), but has experiences more comparable with the adult phenomena of dreams, delusions, hallucinations or, more broadly affective states" (p. 67). One should also examine the protoself theorized by the Portuguese neuroscientist Antonio Damasio (2010). According to Damasio, an initial differentiation between the self and other (the world) as categorically distinct entities does not exist; it is at the moment that the self-experiences the world that a progressive differentiation between self and object begins to take place. Moreover, it should be recalled that the synchrony model for the hypothesis supporting the necessary retention of illusion has not been validated by data based on infant research. In its place, what has been proposed is the separation and reparation model (Tronick and Weinberg, 1997), according to which, it is the reparation of the continuous small interactive separations that normally occur in the caregiver-child relationship that has a positive effect on the healthy development of the child.

According to Milner and Winnicott, it is from the marriage between tongue and nipple, "the first perceptive experience" (Jordan, 1990, p. 433) that internal psychic space develops. These authors brought to our attention the formative importance, for the child's healthy development, of this illusion in early infancy, and the potentially disastrous risks that might arise from a premature, or excessively lengthy, awareness of bodily separateness. As previously stated, Milner hypothesized that the pressure of unsatisfied need may result in the ego's premature (and thus defensive) development. This in turn may result in an inhibition in the original experience of an illusion of oneness, so that the premature transition towards a sense of twoness and the demands matrix of energic potential structures" (Khan, 1960, p. 435). We must emphasize that bodiliness plays a central role in ego formation. One's own body—"that bit of the outer world that is yet also one's self" (Milner, 1977, p. 231)—is the substratum necessary for having experience; it is the basis of the imaginative self (Giannakoulas and Hernandez, 2010). The live subject who experiences a potential space enriches the external reality of something that belongs to his/herself, therefore something not exactly partaking of external reality but which provides it with a metaphorical significance (a metaphor for psychic reality), an original and unique creative contribution, different from anything produced by any other individual.

Turning back at the core question of how it is possible to seek and find the familiar within the unfamiliar, to pass from the primary object to the secondary object, we found Milner's answers from seven perspectives: fantasy, illusion, framework, concentration, absentmindedness, ecstasy, and *rêverie*, all of which represent the facets of one self-same entity. These are seven perspectives that we can identify in our clinical work if we pay attention both to the verbal and non-verbal material, brought by the patient into the here and now of the relationship, and into our countertransference (Stefana, 2015, 2017; Stefana et al., 2021)—seven concepts of which we should avail ourselves in order to study the process of identification, lying at the basis of symbolism.

Fantasy

The first of these concepts is that of fantasy, because only within it can two different objects (or an action and a thought as in the case of opening one's mouth and believing that one is actually speaking) merge into one. Milner (1945) identifies three tightly-linked functions for fantasy: (a) the primitive action substitute, or the conjuring-up function for the satisfying of desire in a hallucinatory way; (b) the primitive knowing or giving meaning to the child's past affective experiences with the object (external happenings that are real, even though subjectively interpreted); (c) the primitive knowing or giving meaning to internal happenings, the experiences of psychic reality such as desires, feelings, and prevailing moods. It follows that the subject must be able to arrive at, even if unconsciously, a minimal differentiation between internal reality and external reality, between subjective and objective—and, at the same time, being able to maintain the omnipotent nature of fantasy (which will establish the roots of symbolic functioning). It should be pointed out that every fantasy does not come about from nothing, but is "built from memory traces of all kinds of sensory experiences, kinaesthetic and visceral as well as visual and auditory" (Milner, 1945, p. 31), and "is what we have made within us out of all past relationships with what is outside, whether they were realised as outside relationships or not" (Milner, 1950, p. 33).

Illusion

The concept of fantasy is however not sufficient. The concept of illusion (that refers to potential space) is also necessary, implying a (fantasy) relationship with an object externally perceived. Milner (1950) conceives the illusion as a necessary means for a healthy adaptation to reality (and for the formation of a true self), rather than a failure of adaptation, because she believes that the existence of the 'me-not-me' boundary is not a question of innate knowledge. It is something that one experiences without awareness, and is something that the child slowly and with difficulty manages to acquire: "our inner dream and outer perception both spring from a common source or primary phase of experience in which the two are not distinguished, a primary 'madness' which all of us have lived through and to which at times we can return" (Milner, 1950, p. 33). Milner—like Winnicott—maintains that the analyst must provide the patient with a space-time in which he/she can create/express his own illusory experiences. She places the sensorial experience of self-object fusion at the basis of the concept of illusion; with the gradual maladjustment of the mother to the needs of the child, what will take place is the progressive development of not only the ability to tolerate frustration and ambivalence but also to make use of transitional phenomena and potential space. Mental space, play space, and symbolization space will be created. In this view, reality may be understood as the result of a "shared illusion [where] everything that is

Such a (mental) malleability is the ability of the therapist-as-object to allow himself/herself to be proof of a 'psychophysical bearing witness' (Hernandez, 2015), to be 'imprinted' (Bertolini, 1999) by the patient, an ability that also comprises the capacity of the therapist-as-container to welcome (Bion, 1962) and to allow himself/herself to be transformed (Milner, 1952b) by the patient's projections. Thus, sometimes, especially with those patients that need the illusion of fusion with the secondary object-therapist, the therapist should allow him/herself to be used as the object of transference, to adapt ourselves to the needs of the patient in order to create the conditions for the continuity of the going-on-being of the analysand, and at the same time to work through and represent this fusional experience. Only afterwards, and also because of the inevitable shortcomings in the therapist's adaptation, will the patient be able to accept the independent existence of the therapist-object, an object that, up until that moment, the patient wished to punish, whenever the object was not malleable enough (or did not live up to his/her fantasy). If this is not the case, then the therapist will be used merely as an object into which the patient projects parts of his/her self, an object incapable of receiving the type of object relation implied in the 'receiving' of a reception (Ogden, 1994). In such phases of the therapeutic process, the ability of the therapist to deal with his/her own negative countertransference (Winnicott, 1949) becomes crucial, thanks to which the patient will: "gradually become able to allow the external object, represented by me, to exist in its own right" (Milner, 1952, p. 194). If the therapist is not capable of therapeutically using the countertransference, he/she may be faced with a projective counteridentification (Grinberg, 1979).

These annotations on the therapist's 'pliability' allow us to glimpse in the background the themes of the therapist's analytic training and authenticity, of collusion in being a 'usable object,' and of the self-referral to the work of the analytic couple in the application of internalized models (elaborated in personal terms or in terms of accommodation to pre-existing lines of thought). In this sense, the autonomy and originality of Milner's path and thought highlight the absolute necessity that the way of doing psychotherapy/psychoanalysis should not be built on a 'false-Self' model or on an ideological knowledge that does not learn from one's own experience in the relationship with that specific patient.

The task of the therapist thus is to provide the 'framed gap' (Milner, 1952a), or, in other words, to create the environmental conditions that will ensure some protection from external intrusions, a protective framework in which the patient's creative experience may take place, in which he/she may be able to ignite his/her imagination in which the secondary object is treated as if it were the primary. Only in this way can the therapist be something else as regards a person in the patient's day-to-day reality. The therapist (the pliable material) and the space-time frame of the setting constitute the 'environmental capacity,' one of the three factors[1] which, according to Milner, play a key role in the process that leads to the recognition of the external world (the not-me), which, in mental health, alternates cyclically with the necessary periodic creative fusion of interacting opposites. In optimal conditions, the therapist can be treated by the patient as a part of himself/herself (illusion of oneness). We are dealing with an experience that, if it comes about together with that of the interpretations provided by the clinician, allows the patient to gradually begin to accept the real attributes of the external world; but up until that moment the space-time limits of the session would also represent a problem for him/her. The analytic setting therefore would have to be a good enough environment for the patient, capable of adequately responding to the patient's needs, and of ensuring hope and promoting its integration (Milner, 1969).

Bollas harks back to the creation of Winnicott's internal potential space and to the frame just described, two elements that allow for a more complete and articulated expression of the transferences, in order to describe the mental neutrality that the analyst should have established in the session, in which it is essential for the analyst to have the ability to sustain doubt and uncertainty (Milner, 1942; Bion, 1970)—a state which allows the patient to manipulate the clinician, through transference usage, into object identity. In fact, Bollas (1987) writes: "By cultivating a freely roused emotional sensibility the analyst welcomes news from within himself that is reported through his own hunches, feeling states, passing images, fantasies, and imagined interpretive interventions. Interestingly, it is a feature of our present day understanding of the transference, that the Other source of the analysand's free association is the psychoanalyst's counter-transference, so much so, that in order to find the patient we must look for him within ourself. This process inevitably points to the fact that there are two 'patients' within the session and therefore two complementary sources of free association" (p. 135).

Milner was also interested in the most internal aspects of the frame, or in the "concentrated states of mind in which one creates one's own inner frame, frame of reference, as essential in all mental productivity, whether creating ideas or works of art, a state in which one holds a kind of inner space" (Milner, 1969, p. 250). She then went as far as tracing the roots of such an ability in the experience of being held in the mother's arms. The frame of which Milner is speaking can therefore also be read as a 'framing' (Bertolini, 2009), in the sense that a patient frames his/her own thoughts when there is a particular state, which is what it is, not for its intrinsic characteristics, but really for the fact that it is the patient framing it. Thus, during the moments of the session in which the patient modifies his/her mode of expression (by slowing it down, lowering the volume, etc.), or the quality of play, it might be helpful to ask ourselves what is going on (in relation to us and the patient), since it could represent the 'birth' of transference. What often happens, however, is that the patient, in session with us, talks or plays, even a great deal, but without framing, or without 'integrating' something that has actual affective value for him/her. It follows that, with these patients that continue to talk, making us perhaps feel nailed to our chair and impotent, because we could not reach them with our interpretations, it might be useful to ask: "What is the patient's unconscious intention in restraining me?" To be able to think of this kind of question while we are with the patient can be very useful because it helps us to ask if the patient is seeking, through us, to transition from his/her primary objects to secondary ones, and, if this is not the case, what could we do to better help him/her. Sometimes it may happen that a simple intervention on our part, in which we verbalize to the patient our sense that he is talking but perhaps not saying anything, could unblock the situation.

At this point we would like to touch on another aspect of the therapeutic process, one closely linked to what has been previously stated. Often patients bring into the session personal material permeated with thoughts and feelings that however can also be very different to what we are experiencing in the here and now of the interaction. In these situations, it would make sense to ask in the here and now of the session: "Who is speaking? To whom is this person speaking? What is the patient talking about and why now?" (Paula Heimann), "How do I feel? Why do I feel like this? Why in this exact moment?" (Margaret Little), and "What is being revealed?" "What form is this revelation taking and to what is it connected?" (Wilfred Bion).

Concentration

There is in fact another term that Milner uses to refer to what we have described as 'framing,' and it is precisely that of concentration. It is during the moments in which one frames, or those moments in which one creates an illusion, that everyone is deeply concentrated in this creative activity. Concentration is a psychophysical feeling before a thinking.

In Milner's view, concentration is like discovering an empty space, a sort of 'uterine space' out of which something new can be born. However, the emptiness is not only a space necessary for the creative act. The patient can experience it, even for a long time, as a useless 'empty space,' as well as a space at risk of collapse or invasion by deadly anxieties and primitive terrors that can sink into irreversible depression, owing to the abandonment of reassuring logical and rational thought.

The threat of emptiness can also be experienced by the therapist, especially when treating severely ill patients. In these cases, a strong lifeline for crossing the emptiness is to feel your own breath, weight, and silence (Milner, 1960). (It must be underlined here an important difference between Milner and Bion: where the former, like Winnicott, places the focus on experiencing, the latter places it on thinking). A type of listening that leads us back to presymbolic sensoriality and to those synaesthesic experiences prior to the structuring of logical thought and word (Di

body by the patient, in order to form thoughts about the experience? Such a state of fusion could represent a base upon which to contemplate something, a previously 'unknown thought,' to use Bollas' (1987) term. We are dealing here with a pre-symbolic catalyst to the symbolization process.

It should be here underlined that to really be with the patient and separate, and thus enable exchange and communion, the therapist needs to both identify and dis-identify at the same time—a capacity that Milner possessed to an amazing degree (Phillips, 2023).

Ecstasy

Being completely engaged in creating a creative illusion is experienced by the subject as a state of ecstasy, a psychic reality that represents "an essential phase in adaptation to reality, since it may mark the creative moment in which new and vital identifications are established" (Milner, 1952c, p. 63). This is what is meant when one says that the new-born, in his imaginative scenario, creates the breast (a subjective reality), with the ensuing 'beatific' experience that the union with it implies. The ecstasy therefore has a procedural dimension connected to the activity of creating an illusion. Being fully engaged in creating an illusion is ecstasy. It is like being able to transcend the limits of human capacity and enter into contact with that oceanic capacity to create the world (Rolland, 1927). The term ecstasy is used to mean the emotional experience of creating a substitute to the experience of holding, to the idiom of a mother's care (or better, to the profound experience, involving the whole self, of being supported and embraced), or of the transitioning from the primary to the secondary object. At a somatic or sensation-based level, it might be experienced as a bodily excitement. In this sense "the aesthetic moment constitutes part of the unthought known. The aesthetic experience is an existential recollection of the time when communicating took place primarily through this illusion of deep rapport of subject and object" (Bollas, 1987, p. 32). What characterizes the aesthetic experience is its self-sufficiency, its capacity to be absorbed in itself, of preventing the subject from escaping it, of transitioning to a level of logical-rational knowledge or to a level of practical action (Krieger, 1976). From what has been said, it is clear that the inability to experience moments of ecstasy—owing to the presence of phantasies and anxieties which cannot be tolerated—implies a developmental blockage (Milner, 1969).

Absentmindedness

The processes and non processes described above create a place for experiencing absent-mindedness. For Milner, being absorbed in a state of daydreaming is necessary for creativity.

> Many of the impediments to going forward into living are the result of a failure of the child's environment to provide the necessary setting for such absent-mindedness. For it seems likely that, in this phase of not distinguishing the 'me' and the 'not-me' we are particularly vulnerable to the happenings in the inner life of those nearest to us emotionally.
>
> (Milner, 1950, p. 192)

This area of experience was addressed by Freud (1914) when discussing primary narcissism: "We are bound to suppose that a unity comparable to the ego cannot exist in the individual from the start; the ego has to be developed" (p. 77). However, Freud also supposed the existence from the beginning of an "original reality-ego" (1915, p. 136) able to produce a preverbal feeling of what is real. Subsequently, echoing Freud, Winnicott (1945) postulated "a primary unintegration" of the ego (p. 139), and Klein (1946) added that there exists "a tendency towards integration alternates with a tendency toward disintegration" (p. 100). The early ego reacts to any anxiety of annihilation either in a passive way, by falling into pieces, or in an active (defensive) way by splitting itself, the object, and the relation to it (Klein, 1946).

It seems to us that Milner aimed to get back to that presymbolic contact with reality. This is a state of extreme vulnerability, in which any impingement can set in motion a displacement either towards clinging to objectivity or seeking refuge into subjectivity. Or both, in a split state. It is an extremely unstable situation.

The quest for a state of absentmindedness in a psychother-apeutic setting can therefore stimulate annihilation anxieties. The patient may react to these anxieties by splitting his/her own mind, the object (the analyst), and the relation between them (the work-ing alliance), in order to give some coherence and order to chaos. However, being able to stay in an absentmindedness state, which implies tolerating a lack of meaning, coherence, and order in the self, is what fosters a genuinely creative process. As Winnicott learned right from Milner, "creativity can be destroyed by too great insistence that in acting one must know beforehand what one is doing" (Winnicott, 1951, p. 392). This also implies the potential utility of being able to limit interpretations and leave more room for silence and waiting.

Rêverie

The last aspect we would like to briefly point out is the *rêverie*. It was Milner who first introduced this term in psychoanalysis, which she adopted from Elton Mayo's (1924) book *Revery and Industrial Fatigue.*

In Milner's view, *rêveries* (daydreams, sensations, images) in monotonous work can be conceived as a state produced by the dissociative capacity of the mind, as a going-on-being measure (Winnicott, 1956) to preserve an internal space of freedom and agency when the subject is faced with a frustrating or even dehu-manizing environment. The field of self-other-consciousness is consequently narrowed, as Pierre Janet (1889) clearly pointed out (Cassullo, 2019a, 2019b).

Milner maintains that the spatial-temporal analytic frame provides the analyst and patient the possibility of connecting to a state of *rêv-erie*, in which the boundaries between their egos, identities, and mutual properties are temporarily suspended, and therefore it is impossible to determine who is the owner of a specific sensation, an image, a thought, or, in Jessica Benjamin's terms (2004), who is the *doer* and who is the *done*. The analyst's availability to perceive, feel and think of *unpleasant* sensations and images helps the patient to do the same and, in doing so, to hold by himself his 'first not-me possessions' (Winnicott, 1953). A shared symbolic thinking is built on such sensations and images, produced during the ecstatic moments of fusion. This makes Milner a pioneer for those modern trends that conceptualize the psychoanalytic process as a co-construction[3] of a somatic-semantic field, rather than an imposition of meaning on the patient's communications (Cassullo and Stefana, 2023).

Notes

1 The other two factors are the repeated bodily experiences of the separation-union with the love object and the object of interchange with the world of the not-self (a point also made by Winnicott), and the gradually growing ability to tolerate the difference between the feelings of unity and duality.
2 In Milner's work we can find a substantial re-evaluation of the concept of pre-logical thinking, which continues to perform the function of intervention into reality even after the acquisition of language skills. She also maintains the concept of psychic functionality through the difference and articulation between primary and secondary processes, and between the illusion of union and separation.
3 It is important to underline how such a co-construction is rooted in all the experiences of the patient and not only in what is happening in the "here and now" of the session, as well as in his/her resources and personal "self-curing forces." In this sense, it is a kind of co-construction different from what is supposed in the interpersonal psychoanalysis view.

Chapter 4

Creativity and play in the consulting room

It can be argued that one of Sigmund Freud's great merits was his development of a psychoanalytic technique that offered an optimum space and distance between therapist and patient, establishing a working relationship within this frame based on the capacity of both participants in the analytic dyad to create and maintain a state of illusion and to continue working within it (Khan, 1971). This emphasis on illusion within analytic space and process has subsequently been enriched by the contribution of a number of psychoanalysts, most notably Milner and Winnicott (Turner, 2002), whose personal and professional meeting was crucial and creatively stimulating on both sides (Anderson, 2023; Boyle Spelman, 2022; Rodman, 2003).

Through studying Milner's works, both youth and adult therapy can be understood as based upon the imaginative scenarios of patient and therapist as well as upon the success of the therapist in helping the patient find meaning in them. To set this process of working through in motion, the therapist should be able to ask themself, taking into account their countertransference, what the imaginative scenario is that the patient is trying to make him or her experience (Stefana, 2017). At the same time, the patient unconsciously grapples with the question of whether and how the therapist can allow aspects of the patient's self to live within them. Such scenarios consist not only of the patient's imaginings about the therapist, but also, simultaneously, of scenarios imagined by the therapist from their own perspective that include speculation on what particularly the patient may be imagining about them.

DOI: 10.4324/9781003330332-5

This is where psychoanalysis lies: in the point of contact between what patient and analyst envisage. Of course, considerable risks of projection lie within this process, especially when the patient's difficulties are on a pre-oedipal and pre-verbal level (Britton et al., 2006). Thus, the therapist should not discard the projective identifications coming from the patient. These show, through interpretation, that the patient has made the therapist a repository for the projection of intolerable mental states, involving their needs, desires, feelings and so on. If the therapist rejects the patient's offerings, the defences against confusion between patient's own and their caregiver's unconscious anxieties and conflicts could be reinforced (defences implying great difficulties in recognizing own emotions and discerning others' ones) and the therapist would not then be facilitating the ego's normal capacity to permit a con/fusion of 'me' and 'not-me,' to achieve a structural de-differentiation, which is a basic element in the development of symbolization and a premise of the *Nachträglichkeith* (i.e., deferred action, *après-coup*).

Emotional experiences within the analytic encounter

Milner (1952b, 1969), alongside Winnicott (1971b), suggests that we should consider the analytic setting not just as symbolization, that is not just as a metaphor for the parent–child relationship in which the latter can introject the therapist's healing modalities (holding, handling and object-presenting), but more precisely as an intense affective experience, in which the therapist becomes a 'transformational object' for the patient, as Christopher Bollas (1987) underlines. Analytic work, therefore, aims to promote the patient's regression to states that precede differentiation, in order to work through them so that a process of development can take place or be resumed. In short, the goal of this benign regression is to reach what Michael Balint (1932, 1936) calls a 'new beginning,' requiring the attainment of a state of 'primary love' (Balint, 1960), or rather the desire to build a dual unity through bodily contact.

In psychotherapy, the experience of fusion with the unfamiliar object or the unfamiliar relationship renders it familiar rather than disturbing, friendly enough to help the child overcome fears and to achieve knowledge of the realities of detachment and separation, along with experiencing the anxiety that these involve. Moreover, this fusion facilitates access to creativity, understood as an act in which one faces reality without preconceptions or a priori constructs (Milner, 1956b). Following this idea, the fundamental capacity of psychic creativity (the ability to form and utilize symbols) involves the necessity of being able to find the familiar in the unfamiliar. To establish object relations there needs to be a process made possible by:

> the basic identifications which (…) require an ability to tolerate a temporary loss of sense of self, a temporary giving up of the discriminating ego which stands apart and tries to see things objectively and rationally and without emotional colouring.
>
> (Milner, 1952b, p. 97)

If the patient allows him or herself to let go and have an experience of their imaginative landscape as concrete and real within the analytic relationship, they will also allow unconscious emotional elements to enter consciousness, and thus may perhaps be able to achieve their assimilation into the functioning of the self.

The creation of an illusion requires profound concentration on the part of the patient, which initially involves a feeling, before becoming a thought. This represents a discovery of empty space that is not only the necessary space for the creative act; it can also be a place of distress and terror, a feeling of falling into irreparable depression, owing to the loss of reassuring rational thought. We have to become able to address this void, and our lifeline across it is our breath, the awareness of our weight, the silence and so on (see Milner, 1960), or rather a type of listening that leads us back to pre-verbal sensoriality and to those synaesthesic experiences prior to the structuring of logical thought and word (Di Benedetto, 1991). Milner (1952b, 1956b) believes that concentrating on the generation of a creative illusion involved the ecstatic experience of establishing new and vital identifications. Here, we can note an important difference between Milner and Winnicott, on the one hand, and Bion, on the other. Where the former two analysts focused on experiencing, the latter focused more on thinking.

As an example, let us think of a child who creates the secondary object, according to his imaginative scenario. The child will dedicate himself to this illusion, involving the passage from the primary to the secondary object, at least while conceiving it; in other words, while living in a state of ecstasy, produced by the subjective reality of what is created. However, during a session, the therapist or analyst may wish on some occasions to interrupt the concentration, the playing, the ecstasy of the patient, in order to bring them back to logical thought. Milner asks herself, more insistently than others did, what the usefulness of this diversion of attention was. She arrived at the conclusion that there was none, in that, as she saw it: "the logical terms in which the capacity for symbol formation is thought about are perhaps less important than the pre-logical. I want to suggest that it is the terms in which we think, on the deeper non-verbal levels of the psyche, about this specifically human capacity for making symbols that in part determines the way the capacity works in us" (Milner, 1957, p. 217). Thus, when the patient is concentrated on creating an illusion, there should be no interruptions; they should not be made to emerge prematurely from this creative activity. It is up to us clinicians to tolerate the diversion from our Aristotelian logic (designing the excluded middle principle according to which a thing is *or* is not, rather than be *and* not be simultaneously), by accommodating the patient's concentration.

Reporting on part of a session with her patient Simon, eleven years old, Milner says: "he would say, 'What is your name?' and I would have to say, 'What is my name?' Then he would answer with the name of some chemical, and I would say, 'What is there about that?' And he would answer, 'it's lovely stuff, I've made it!'" (Milner, 1952b, p. 99). For this child, the phrase 'your name is gas' was a symbolic equation (Segal, 1950).

The need to reflect on the possibility of feeling excluded is a specific part of our work with patients. This reflection can lead to an awareness of the necessity of being able to feel excluded, namely to allow the patient to exclude our 'white coat' and to ask a patient could be very useful, because it helps us ask ourselves if the patient is attempting, through us, to pass from his/her primary to his/her secondary objects and, whenever it is not so, what we could do to better assist the process. Milner suggests that we pay attention to the possibility that when the patient is talking about a friend, a teacher or an aunt, he or she could unconsciously have in mind the passage from the primary to the secondary object.

Anna Margarida Chagas Bovet, an Italian analyst of Brazilian origins, clearly illustrates the extent to which Milner suggests to the therapist to not take for granted, at a certain point, the patient's capacity for play, since underlying the willingness to engage in this activity, the patient's continued struggle with the painful work of constructing a shared reality may be found (Chagas Bovet, 1997, 1999). The spatial-temporal trustworthiness, characteristic of the setting, makes possible the development of a sense of continuity, both within the patient's self, and within his or her relationship with the therapist, in the context of the potential space essential to the capacity for play, which has not been developed enough in the patient's primary relationship. The patient's needs can therefore demand that during play—a pre-logical and creative activity—we clinicians accept becoming part of the patient's self, created by him, an omnipotent illusion that we ought to sustain until alterity is no longer tolerable. In this way, the psychic work of the therapeutic dyad takes the form of a separation-individuation process. In situations where the state of the illusion of unity cannot be worked through, but is only confirmed in a concrete sense, in the transference there may be a repetition with collusive elements, understood as the basis of separation anxiety.

The role of illusion in symbol formation

In life, there are moments, recurring and circumscribed, found both in children, as Winnicott identified, as well as adults, where there is a temporary renouncing of differentiation, where boundaries dissolve and Aristotelian logic loses its meaning. Milner

(1950), following her personal search into the inability to paint, suggests that it is exactly in these moments of primary 'madness', that every man creates new symbols, attributing a personal and subjective meaning to the reality just built, as "the substance of experience is what we bring to what we see, without our own contribution we see nothing" (p. 33). The importance of these moments is evident, for example, in autistic people, during whose infancy these kinds of oscillations might have not occurred (Tustin, 1994).

Milner makes the idea of 'primary imagination' described by the English poet and philosopher Samuel Taylor Coleridge (1817) her own: "the living power and prime agent of all human perception, and as a repetition in the finite mind of the eternal act of creation in the infinite I AM" (Milner, 1952b, p. 159), she writes. She makes this idea hers, by speaking of "the original 'poet' in each of us" (pp. ivi, 88). Let us remember that the poetic mind is an unconscious mind, where the pre-logical operates, and through which the imagination manages to feel within itself, embodying the I AM. In those moments where one struggles for independence, the unthinkable illusion of "a separation that is not a separation" takes shape, the creative illusion that forms the individual's integrated experience (Milner, 1977, p. 247).

Milner, after long reflection, conceptualized imagination, viewing it as a feeling of being in someone else's shoes, meaning that one treats the secondary object, when engaged with it, as if it were the primary object, through imagination.

On the subject of imagination, Winnicott (1970) has shown us that a sign of health in the mind can be traced to the ability to enter imaginatively into the thoughts and feelings of another, without becoming submerged in them or overwhelmed by them, while at the same time allowing the other to do the same with us. In clinical terms, if one of her patients were to experience a psychotic delirium, we think that Milner would not try to flatten or erase their experience of it. Rather, she would probably feel that she should familiarize herself with the mental processes—the 'logic'—of the patient having this experience. What interests her is the question of why the patient was imagining something. This capacity to tolerate disillusionment. One can glimpse in this attitude an important quality that a good parent should possess: knowing how to correct one's inevitable errors, in an attempt to make sense of and satisfy the needs of the child, especially when one is dealing with the complexity of the pre-verbal mind, in which such needs and desires are strongly felt, but often without the child knowing what they consist of, and of course not being able to express them clearly. It is obvious that the aforementioned interpretation was not about unveiling the 'certain meaning' of an unconscious fantasy. Rather, it seemed to be a proposal, an exploration, allowing the analyst to gather information, which they later had to work through, on the patient's self, taking also into account the modifications generated by the emotional and relational meanings attributed by the patient to the same interpretation.

For Milner (1956a, 1973), what makes the experience of both patient and therapist sterile, is the inability to maintain doubt, that is the experience of emptiness, and/or the failure to integrate the knowing for masculine assertive consciousness, with the keeping to the feminine feelings, two aspects which are both necessary for good listening and for a deep journey into oneself.

Often patients, during sessions, relive and re-actualise certain events of their lives. The task of the therapist, through the creation and maintenance of the analytical setting, including their own internal makeup, is to provide, inasmuch as they are capable, a type of connection, a situation of 'total active adaptation,' gradual enough in its decrease and subsequent disappearance to be a good enough environment, capable, therefore, of adequately satisfying needs, of ensuring separation, and of promoting integration (Milner, 1969).

Milner states:

> Certainly there is discontinuity between early body memories and later experience (...) [and] interpretations in terms of splitting do not carry conviction or start psychic growth to begin again on the level where the deepest hold-up of development is operative (...) [a] hold-up [that] seems to lie partly

in an inability to establish the necessary oscillation between, on the one hand, a state of diffuse being in which there are no boundaries, only fluidity.

My own clinical experience does lead me to agree with the idea that the ability to find objects with whom relationship can be made does depend on the previous existence of a recurrent state of unity, one which comes originally from the mother-child fusion. Also that this feeling of unity is not a projective identification resulting from splitting a pre-existent ego, but is the result of recurrent awareness, in feeling, of an undifferentiated state of no separation, a state described by Masud Khan (…) in terms of 'a pre-stage of infancy development where ego and id themselves emerge from an undifferentiated matrix of energic potential structure.'

(Milner, 1960, p. 238)

Milner speaks here about accommodating the patient's need, within the setting established by analysis, in order to promote a type of experience that did not take place enough during the initial phases of the patient's life, thus not allowing the start of a good enough process of development.

The use of the therapist-object and the end of psychoanalytic treatment

Again, regarding Simon, Milner (1952b) wrote:

With this boy there was always the question of whether to emphasise, in interpreting, the projection mechanisms and persecutory defences and to interpret the aggression as such; but when I did this the aggression did not seem to lessen and I was sometimes in despair at its quite implacable quality. (…) But when I began to think along the lines described above [which means abandoning the idea of showing the patient his aggressive impulses and taking charge of one's own negative countertransference], even though I knew that I was not succeeding in putting these ideas clearly into words in my interpretations, the aggression did begin to lessen and the continual battle over the time of the beginning of each session disappeared.103)

In this clinical example, we can see how Milner realizes that, in order to be open to the patient's need for contact, she had to abandon interpretations, at least until integration had been achieved, in favour of making herself totally present during the sessions. Something similar occurred in another case by Milner (1969), the analysis of her patient Susan. As we better see in the next chapter, this psycho-physical presence enabled Milner to take charge of her own negative countertransference. This is an idea that Winnicott (1949) famously dealt with in his listing of a series of reasons for which a mother hates her own baby. Winnicott concluded that if a mother cannot tolerate hating her baby, the child will suffer in their later development. The good enough therapist is the one who can love a patient, while hating him or her at the same time. This is necessary, in order to avoid the development of a negative countertransference, which would be difficult to recognize. According to Winnicott (1949), the therapist should be able to accept ambivalence towards his/her own patient, allowing the patient to tyrannize him/her, knowing that he/she will not be destroyed (except in the patient's fantasy).

On this subject, Winnicott (1969) wrote:

> The subject says to the object: 'I destroyed you', and the object is there to receive the communication. From now on the subject says: 'Hullo object!' 'I destroyed you.' 'I love you.' 'You have value for me because of your survival of my destruction of you.' 'While I am loving you I am all the time destroying you in (unconscious) fantasy'.
>
> (p. 713)

The attainment of objective hate, defined as 'legitimate' by André Green (1977), that the patient goes in search of, is a necessary condition for the feeling of objective love. From the patient's point of view, the object—the therapist—survives when they more or less stay the same, not reacting with rejection or punishment to the patient's aggression, fed by projective mechanisms and persecutory defences. Through this experience, the patient can achieve a recognition of a sense of self and of external reality. This profoundly influences technique, inasmuch as it allows one to go beyond protecting the patient. This is a fundamental point in the theories of both Winnicott and Milner. They refer to this idea as the 'use of the object:' after having established a relationship of omnipotence, what becomes necessary is a phase in which the object (analyst), no longer under the patient's omnipotent control, may be destroyed by the subject in his unconscious fantasy; we are not dealing here with a manifestly open destructiveness but with destructiveness in fantasy. This need to destroy the gratifying object, demonstrated by Winnicott (1969), further stimulated in Milner a bonding process with her own reflections on primary omnipotence and the intensity of the trauma of disillusionment, regarding the sheer incredulity and the abysmal depth of dread that can come from the forced renunciation of one's own omnipotence, owing to a failure of the environment in a moment in which the ego is not strong enough to tolerate it: "when it has even been feeling, not only that it was king of the castle but also that it was both king and castle itself" (Milner, 1977, p. 284). It should be mentioned here that Milner was already using in her clinical work the concepts of patient's use of the object and analyst's non-retaliatory survival while Winnicott was still working on in the 1960s (Bruggen, 2023).

Milner linked the ways in which one achieves recognition of the sense of self and of external reality to bodily concentration[1] more than to primary aggression or destructiveness, as indicated by Winnicott (1950). In therapy, the subject is able to destroy the therapist inside him or herself, by fantasizing about not coming anymore to sessions, or, for example, by telling him/herself that he/she cannot listen to anything said by the object. Only by surviving can the environment-object be used by the subject, who will then become able to see the world objectively. It is the experience of being held that makes the illusion of unity possible and it is the inevitable end of the session that creates the

her to broaden her view to what lies around the symptom, the individual communication or drawing, in order to search for its internal logic and its entanglements. It is a somewhat 'divergent gaze,' the same one that was at the root of her youthful interest in the Montessori school, in which children's creativity and their possibilities are facilitated in their expression, rather than constrained by the rigid canons of an adultomorphing and castrating school. Milner's approach has an almost 'naturalistic' focus (certainly related to her training in general psychology and her observational spirit cultivated from her youth) on what happens around her and beyond her gaze.

Although antecedent in terms of time and biography to Milner's entry into the psychoanalytic world, the aforementioned research on learning difficulties can already be read as a reflection on psychic functioning. The latter is understood not only in terms of cognitive functioning, but also, and especially, in experiential terms, both on a personal and environmental level. As if to say that 'manifest content' explains too little of an individual's psychic world if it is not contextualized within an environment and history that needs to be sought and allowed to emerge. By allowing and facilitating patients to express themselves and be themselves, it is possible to come to discover stories within stories and see images in verbal communications (Kleimberg, 2019, 2023).

This position centred on the search for 'what is missing' or 'what is unclear' (from which the whole theme of accepting 'non-knowledge' and capacity for doubt develops) is not experienced as a state of personal uncertainty or disorientation, nor does it generate a kind of defensive tension to acquiring knowledge. Rather, it is a firm determination to give up fantasies about the supposed self-sufficiency of one's knowledge, in order to discover what lies beyond it. Such an attitude rests on a good knowledge of one's own territory (which includes psychoanalytic theories of reference, but also one's knowledge of art, literature, and general culture) and awareness of its boundaries, and the certainty that there is more beyond such boundaries. The appeal to the hidden of the Unconscious and its truths is immediate here. What is missing, and then emerges, becomes transformative not because it fills a gap (in fact, it does not respond to an accumulative need as much as to an ability to invest in the other-than-self), but because it leads to change one's thoughts, to discover new boundaries and identities. This makes it possible to find and take differentiating paths that allow the search for what is outside of oneself.

It is the same unconscious that gives signs of existence in the analysis room and provides Milner with material to realize that her interpretations, while theoretically correct, are not only not transformative but sometimes even exasperating. She realizes that she does not understand what deep message the patient intends to communicate and, consequently, her interpretations do not meet it.

This need to go 'beyond' can be found, in a systematic way, in Milner's relationships with her various interlocutors, but first and foremost, and in an epistemologically lucid way, it can be found in the prudence she intends to have about her own thinking. A prudence that shows itself in the form of her frequent 'it seems to me.'[1] This way of saying can be read as an element of caution, certainly legitimate and very appreciable in terms of humility and deontological rigour. At the same time, it can also be read as an element of problematization which actively tends toward confrontation, since it is not enough to take what we consciously know we know as definitive. In this sense of seeking the 'outside of oneself,' aimed at the acquisition of a more complex vision, Milner's act of showing to acquaintances and colleagues the drawings of patient Susan and asking them for their personal judgement should be read (Milner, 1955).

In more general terms, the analysis of Milner's texts reveals an epistemological awareness that brings her closer to a Popperian reflection on the limits of an approach based on inductivism and the implicit deductivism of all our theoretical-clinical hypotheses, with an almost falsificationist approach and the use of abductive logic.

Milner (1944) writes:

> I came to the conclusion that in fact I could not prove my hypothesis at all from the material, for though the material in the analysis may seem to provide convincing proof, for the analyst conducting it, of the truth of his theory, for anyone

else I think it can only provide illustration of the theory. I think this must be so, since the material presented to anyone else must always be a selection from the great richness of varieties of behaviour (including gestures, manner, tones of voice) and must therefore always be selected on the basis of some theory; thus one can never prove that one's selection of the material is unbiased and that one has not omitted other facts which would prove some different theory.

(p. 16)

Clinical work: Milner and Susan in a 20-year treatment

Susan was a girl with severe psychotic disorder, who was 23 years old at the beginning of treatment. She was a person with a childhood history of severe traumatization within an early and prolonged symbiotic relationship with a schizogenic and inconsistently seductive mother. When her mother died, Susan had a breakdown and was hospitalized where, after a few months, she also underwent electroconvulsive therapy. Three weeks after electroconvulsive therapy—this was in 1943—she arrived at Milner's office saying she had lost her soul and that the world was no longer outside her.

Susan lived as a guest in the home of Donald Winnicott and his wife (referred to as Mr and Mrs X in Milner's text) for seven years during her analytic treatment, which Winnicott himself supervised, and for which he bore the financial burden (Milner, 1969; see also Hughes, 1989).

During the first seven years of treatment, Milner used a classical psychoanalytic technique (i.e., early interpretations of transference and unconscious contents) to which, however, Susan did not respond with any improvement. At these time, all that Milner (1969) often can do seem:

> to be to sit quietly 'holding' her, warmly, in my attention, which was not always easy, as this phase of depletion, lack of all hope, was often defended against by a spikey anger with me; but even though what I actually said in these sessions did not seem to reach her at all.

(p. 75)

Then, suddenly, from 1950, Susan began to doodle and bring her drawings (over 4,000 by the end of therapy) to her therapist, who accepts them gratefully and treasures them. Milner realizes that through drawing Susan was:

> constantly creating a bridge between me and herself, a basis for communication, since I believed her drawings did all have meaning potentially; even if I did not as yet understand more than a small part of them I had at least made the attempt to relate them to what had gone on between us during the years. Thus these so many bits of herself that she had given me had, I thought, been modified by my capacity to see her as a whole continuing person, even if she could not yet see herself or me as that.
>
> (Milner, 1969, p. 303)

Beginning with Susan's drawing, continued internal probing into herself during sessions, and more general leanings towards understanding the patient's experiences, Milner gradually (co-)creates a technique effective in facilitating Susan to experience—and internalize—a symbiotic link with her. A link that, unlike the one with her biological mother, is now with an empathic/reliable/consistent object. The relationship with the therapist allows Susan to internalize the benign experience and gradually strengthen a differentiating self and eventually achieve a separate existence. The treatment ends twenty years after its inception, a period during which Susan manages to go from being so disturbed that she could not even walk a few steps down the street unaccompanied, to being married and maintaining a stable job.

One of the reasons Milner did not deviate from the classical technique for years, despite the fact that it seemed to yield no positive therapeutic results, is that:

> It became an intensely rich symbol, too, of what I felt I had to become able to achieve in myself, while with her in sessions, if I were to help the healing process to start functioning again in the area of her deepest splits—especially the mind-body split. Thus it was here that I had to think once more about my own capacity to achieve, knowingly, a partially

undifferentiated and indeterminate state, in her sessions, to hold in myself a blankness, an empty circle, emptiness of ideas, not always pushing myself to try and find an interpretation. And how difficult this still was! I thought again of how constantly she would produce in me a feeling of empty-headedness, the feeling of nothing to say; and how I still fought against this feeling, or sometimes used it as a basis of interpretations to do with her envy of me, her wish to make my brain impotent, uncreative, like the devil 'crushing under foot what isn't his.' But I remembered, too, how interpretations of this kind had not seemed to produce any psychological movement.

(p. 253)

Classical theory and technique

In Milner's disposition towards going beyond there is room for the contributions (in terms of dreams, drawings, play activities, behavior, words, etc.) of her patients, if only insofar as the analyst is able to reflect on them by reading them not always or not only as resistances, but also as deeper communications which convey archaic parts of the self or that are related to the need to establish a different relationship between what is felt as reality and what is not felt as such. This is what Milner (1969) describes as the vital contribution of patients:

Certainly, some patients seemed to be aware, dimly or increasingly, of a force in them to do with growth, growth towards their own shape, also as something that seemed to be sensed as driving them to break down false inner organizations which do not really belong to them; something which can also be deeply feared, as a kind of creative fury that will not let them rest content with a merely compliant adaptation; and also feared because of the temporary chaos it must cause when the integrations on a false basis are in the process of being broken down in order that a better one may emerge.

(p. 431)

In the first seven years of treatment, Milner repeatedly notes how her own 'classic' interpretations (those based on Oedipal issues, aspects of identification and projection, or persecutory anxieties), while maintaining their coherence and validity, are often not mutative/therapeutic. At the base of the technical choice of those interpretations is the thought that she must stick to the analyst's task of trying to give back to the patients what they seemed to be telling her, "translating it into discursive logical statements, like 'This is what you are really feeling (…) but are denying it because (…) etc., etc.'" (Milner, 1969, p. xxxix). During the early years of treatment, Milner had thought of Susan's acute depression and interpreted it in terms of identification with the mother's depleted and unrefillable breast. Although the patient did not reject such interpretations, there was no evidence that they led to any psychic improvement. More generally, Milner (1969) found herself:

> constantly swinging between the sense of a compulsion to feed her with attempted 'good' verbalizations of what I thought she was unconsciously feeling, and the sense, more profoundly felt but too often and too easily lost sight of, that I must stick to trying to direct her attention to the various ways in which she was preventing her own creative forces getting to work on the problem.
>
> (p. 48)

Essentially, several of such classical interpretations often 'are of no use to' or 'produce so little effect on' non-neurotic patients. Moreover, such interpretations may give rise to intense resentment in the patient. In Susan, such resentment is provoked by feeling robbed of the residual power to take care of herself, which is necessary to feel that she exists as a person (not as someone else's object), and that she has value. According to Milner, this situation signifies a kind of stalemate in transference development, and the patient's perception of any improvement, as an admission of the horror of what she believes she has done in the past.

An intervention aimed at clarification and relief, which would theoretically be appropriate in certain clinical situations, can thus be experienced as manipulative and destructive in others. It is when a patient brings a lot of meaningful material to the session and describes extreme emotional states, but transference interpretations do not yield positive effects, that the therapist should pay more attention to her own experience in the here and now of the session. She might thus find that she is kept completely out of the picture of the analytic situation made by the patient. At a countertransference level, Milner sometimes feels that she is not present in the session with Susan and sometimes that the patient is not, either. Consistently, Susan feels that "neither she nor I was there" (Milner, 1969, p. 71).

Somehow, Susan leads Milner to repeatedly question her own clinical mode of action. Milner thus comes to the realization of the importance of playing not only a translator role, which with this psychotic patient does not produce the expected results, but also a reparatory/nutritive role. She points out how these ideas remained below the threshold of her consciousness for many years. She glimpsed them when, for brief moments, they surfaced, but not well enough or long enough to adhere to them consistently as clinical principles to work on. Hence, she found herself continuing "to work too hard for her, be too busy trying to find 'explanations' instead of patiently trying to find the conditions under which new experiences would become possible for her" (Milner, 1969, p. 57). This 'too active' work that Milner was doing, supported a collusion of the analytic couple, in which Milner did not interpret the image of omnipotence that Susan constantly tried to attribute to her.

Milner notices a feature of the functioning of the analytical couple, namely that what they "were faced with was a defect in her thinking, one connected with the relation between the articulate and inarticulate forms and phases of it" (Milner, 1969, p. 89). It is precisely Susan's intense difficulties in making her own any interpretation that depends on the search for a hidden symbolic meaning in something she has brought to the session which allows Milner to have a first awareness of any kind of defect in Susan's thinking. Therefore, it was useless to give this type of interpretation, "as long as she had not achieved enough of dualistic vision to recognize that there can be unconscious wishes and fantasies as well as conscious ones" (1969, p. 104). The persistence of such a situation in which what appears to be appropriate interpretations do not have any positive effect, leads Milner and Susan to "mutually agreed that the analysis could be looked upon only as a failure, so far as the symptom was concerned, and had better stop" (Milner, 1950, p. 55).

A paradigm shift: the importance of not knowing

Adopting a problematizing approach, Milner formulates alternative hypotheses to classical psychoanalysis to break the impasse in the therapeutic process. Thus, when Susan responds to her interpretations by constantly telling her that she (Milner) is a fool, she no longer reads it as neurotic resistance. Milner now senses that there is something more complex and strange going on in the analytic couple, and she begins to visualize a different scenario, where her comments can acquire clinical concreteness. Milner takes note of what Freud wrote: the patient heals:

> only if we have aroused in him representations of such expectations as can agree with reality. What was inapplicable in the assumptions of the physician falls away during the course of the analysis; it must be withdrawn and replaced by something more nearly correct.
>
> (Freud, 1917, p. 452)

She comes to understand that:

> there might have been a more dynamic result if I had been able to point out to her her intolerance of my not knowing and having to wait for knowledge of what to say to emerge. If I had said this I think I might have laid the ground for talking about the recurrent phase of 'not-knowing' in the rhythm of all creative activity; a phase that she seemed to me to be persistently rejecting, and thus cutting herself off from her inner creative source of repair and growth. Thus I came to see that many of my interpretations at that time were defences against my own 'not knowing' and therefore were felt by

her as presumptuous attacks on her own creative processes, attacks which only strengthened the impregnability of her psychic armour.

(Milner, 1969, p. 49)

At a more abstract level, Milner is suggesting that words, which in the course of development come to become the primary means of expression for most sufficiently mentally healthy adult persons, constitute a bridge between internal and external reality. However, they can become entangled in the original confusion between these two realities, which is why they should not be given absolute value.

Starting from the delight in verbal nonsense (Milner, 1942) related to the relief of escaping the false dominance of words,[2] in an attempt to better understand Susan's communications and adapt to her functioning, Milner problematizes both the content and form of her own clinical communications.

From this new perspective, the drawings that Susan began to bring into session beginning in 1950 take on a different and deeper value because they recall the indeterminacy and ineffability of some of the states of mind. They are "beyond the reach of words used logically and discursively" (Milner, 1969, p. xi). Accordingly, Milner makes some changes in technique to accommodate what seem to her to be Susan's particular needs and difficulties. She centres the narrative on the drawings, seeing them as containing, in a highly condensed form, the essence of what the analytic couple is trying to understand. She comes to see the drawings as the patient's private language, which anyone who wants to help her must learn to read and 'speak.'

This patient's private language, which can take shape even without the patient's own knowledge, is well represented in many of Milner's comments on Susan's drawings. Particularly significant is the "Profile Madonna" drawing (Milner, 1955, Fig. 31 p. 117; 1969, Fig. 57, p. 221) that shows:

a female head enclosed in a rather sinister-looking shadow-like multiple profile, covered with a kind of helmet made of spikey breast shapes. Below are three circles which overlap and I notice that here again is the alternating symbol; as one looks at the circles they seem to be either two faces in profile with a tiny bit that is in common for both, or one full face in the centre. There are also spikey breast shapes radiating downwards all round and one very black spiked shape on the right, like a shield, but which also attacks. Here it seems to me that the lower half of the pictures carried on the problem of where is she to be.

(Milner, 1969, p. 220)

Wrote Milner:

I have also tried to show ways in which I have come to make use of the symbols Susan offered me, not only the oscillating profiles, but also a simpler form, that shown in the centre of Figure (…) the overlapping of two circles, and use it as the basis of a model for thinking about the relation between two persons, about the need for an area of overlap in which there is a partial fusion of interest, a bit of common ground.

(Milner, 1950, p. 108)

Susan's "Profile Madonna" drawing, like many others, becomes a multidimensional tool of communication and at the same time a communication in its own right. It is a:

- communicative code (iconic vs. linguistic, bodily *vs.* verbal);
- communication on content (the multiple coexisting identities);
- communication about the relationship (as a pliable medium for both);
- shared experience;
- experience of creativity (in the freedom to subjectively interpret the themes of the drawing itself);
- experience of integration;
- communication about boundaries, distance, conflict, and fusion;
- expression of something one knows without knowing to know it; and

- communication about the world of reality and the world of imagination.[3]

Staying on a plane that on the surface could be described as 'more linguistic,' Milner makes changes in her methodology of working with Susan based on what seemed to be her particular needs and difficulties.

> Instead of trying to put into words for her what I considered to be the unconscious phantasy causing the anxiety of the moment, I began trying to keep her to the point of herself seeking to find an exact word for what she was feeling. Thus, when she said, as she often did, 'Oh, it's useless, it's impossible to describe,' I would try to show her how she seemed to be putting a rigid barrier between the describable and the indescribable.
>
> (Milner, 1987a, p. 51)

This operation is not without risks, since it involves going beyond a shared psychoanalytic thought to seek personal paths by not giving up one's knowledge and not sacrificing one's autonomy and originality. Milner speaks of the fatigue in her own counter-transference, sometimes irritated and tiring, her tendency to do too much, to overfill Susan. This also raises in Milner the problem of how to connect areas of her own personal and clinical experience with currently accepted psychoanalytic theories or with revised theories (to approximate clinical experiences) which are acceptable to the psychoanalytic mainstream. That is, how to justify the change in technique in terms of psychoanalytic technique theory?

> All this time I was hearing much talk from analysts about the need for constant interpretation of the many subtle ways in which patients seek, unconsciously, to control the analyst and the analysis. However, talking to Susan about such matters only plunged her into a deeper despair, even a state in which all contact between us seemed to be lost. I thought this was not surprising, considering the great lacks in her mother's capacity to adapt to, that is, to be controlled by, her child's needs. In fact I was coming to think more and more about an infant's primary need for the illusion of omnipotence, made

possible through the mother's adaptation, if the necessary
disillusion and recognition of helplessness is to become a
creative reality.

(Milner, 1969, p. 129)

Thus, it is necessary to abandon the primacy of words and the
analyst's single-person view, and open up to other, not exclusively
verbal, forms of communication. The direction indicated by
Milner is to overcome the false opposition between 'work' and
'play,' based on an adultomorphic (Peterfreund, 1978) assumption.
In clinical practice, this means asking the adult patient to say—or
the child patient to do—whatever they feel like saying or doing
(see Ogden, 2016, 2018), in order to better understand what
patients are trying to communicate in the context of how they see
the meaning of their lives. It actually means helping the patient to
play with words/toys/drawings.

It should be noted that the change in technique also includes the
use in analysis of the ~4,000 drawings made by Susan outside of her
sessions, material that has in part found its place inside the session
and, even more, inside the analyst's mind. A further aspect of the
change lies in the fact that these drawings are gifts from Susan to
the analyst, which the latter accepts with gratitude and treasure.
This exchange opens up a change from the classical analytic setting, where gifts can more easily represent enactments, and as
such they are interpreted by the analyst. If there is 'exchange,' this
is in terms of verbal exchanges, of mutual presence, while the
more concrete element that passes from the patient to the therapist
is the fee. In this case, the interpretation brings back to a symbolic
register what the patient—with her own autonomous change of
communicative code—has expressed in concrete terms.

In Milner's action, on the other hand, the shift of a shared code
is present, operating both out of the need to respect Susan's
defences, and also in order to communicate with her within
Susan's (conscious and unconscious, symbolic and concrete, personal and relational) registers of signification, avoiding disposses-
sing her and stripping her of her utterly personal idiom.[4] It could
be said—with a contemporary language, suited for contemporary

patients—that she was able to operate a cultural decentralization, as in the paradigm of transcultural psychology and psychotherapy.

Such reciprocity in giving and taking implies a status of equality between Milner and Susan which allows Susan not to consider herself entirely useless (Gorer, 1970). In fact, Milner sees her drawings also as "a touching that was reparative, not just a way of seeking comfort in loneliness, but seeking to do reparation for all her destructive intentions or actions" (1969, p. 267).

It thus becomes even clearer why for Milner drawings are something quite different from a more or less naive mode of expression. The drawings are points of connection.

> In spite, however, of all these other meanings that I saw in her act of making and bringing me the drawings, I did feel that their primary function was, as I have said, to serve as a kind of bridge towards her acceptance of this 'otherness' of the external world; through the very fact that they had real existence in the outer world and at the same time, in their content and their form, came entirely from herself and her inner world, they were a non-discursive affirmation of her own reality.
>
> Also, in general I could see them as thus affirming the reality of her own experience by slowly building up, restoring, in symbolic form, all kinds of denied aspects of her infantile bodily relation to her mother, with the accompanying fantasies, including especially all the primitive self-explodings into the world-mother-me that seemed to be partly depicted in her constant use of exploding out-raying forms.
>
> (Milner, 1969, p. 269)

Surrendering to creativity

The dynamics of the therapeutic relationship between Milner and Susan (as well as with Simon or Rachel) show a different functioning than what is described in the patient's personal and family history. Susan had had to adjust to an early growth, developing a reactive sense of adaptation, a need for control, a denial of a personal internal world because she was grappling with an overly demanding and intrusive external world. In the course of the therapeutic journey, it is the external world—or rather, Milner—adapting to Susan's infantile needs, rather than demanding passive adaptation from her.

The analyst's is a "creative surrender" (Ehrenzweig, 1957; Milner, 2012). An ability to surrender, not on a basis of helplessness or incapacity, but as a deliberate letting go of all personal concerns and fuss, allows surrender to become a transformative/developmental act. Thus, this passage does not represent a kind of 'defeat' or weakness, and finds its foundation in the reminder of the need for conflict or—in less charged terms—a differentiation, in which emptiness and nothingness are the premise of any subsequent presence. It also means that in some clinical situations it is necessary to leave unsatisfied the anxious impulse to logically organize the material brought by the patient and tolerate an unorganized and undifferentiated 'mess' phase of how the therapist experiences the relationship with the patient.

With Susan, there are three main points of change introduced by Milner. The first is her being a pliable medium, willing to tolerate a degree of overlap with her (somewhat similar to Simon's use of drawings and toys in his game of war between two villages). The second is the function of being able to hold her in her heart, protecting through an appropriate framework (also made up of silences throughout the session) her experiencing a state of oneness, so that she can later return to a duality. The third element is holding back from expressing in words what is believed to be the unconscious fantasy causing the anxiety of the moment in the patient, to the point where the patient herself tries to find a suitable word to communicate what she is feeling. Indeed, the search for the exact word moves away from an interpretive modification given by the 'other' (i.e., the analyst).

In the synthesis of these statements, some fundamental elements present in both the clinical context and in theorizing emerge: (a) the therapist's analysis of herself as a necessary step in the personal work of understanding; (b) the search for factors that stand in the way, or are outside conscious awareness; and (c) the boundaries of what is or is not in the working frame (or even in the setting, one might say), rather than in the interaction between two people and their areas of fusion and differentiation.

Milner goes out on a limb by recognizing not only the dimension of countertransference, but also the creative contribution that the analyst is called upon to make, even in terms of relinquishing her omnipotent cognitive power. Over the years Milner comes to understand that for there to be real change in patients, especially the most compromised ones, it is not enough to understand more and give better interpretations—although "the art of psychoanalysis is in finding ways of saying sometimes difficult things in a way that people can hear and possibly even enjoy" (Phillips, 2023, p. 64). Such a change in the patient first requires a change in the therapist, that is, the difficult renunciation of striving to provide explanations and put into words unconscious concerns of the patient, even if they are clamoured for by the patient. Milner, therefore, had to learn to watch, let the patient know she was there, and wait for the patient to find her own response.

Milner understands that among Susan's greatest needs are to have continual proof that her therapist ponders about her in her heart and sees her as her own person, and to have an environment (the space-time of the session) in which she does not have to control the external world. Often, Milner says, what can be done is to sit quietly 'holding' the patient warmly, in our attention, which is not always easy since we are often the object of anger or other strong negative emotions. Unlike interpretations, such psycho-physical presence during the encounter seems to reach the patient (through nonverbal channels such as, for example, gaze or an intimate, non-intrusive psycho-physical presence).

At the end of the day, keeping silent also becomes a positive element, because it leaves the therapist and patient some space for not-knowing, and trying to know, each for oneself, and at the same time in collaboration with the other. Gradually Milner (1973) comes to understand that there is a kind of emptiness or absence of perception that can be of value and can be a necessary step in a creative process, like a field left 'fallow' (Khan, 1977).

The vital impulse and the contribution of the patient

Milner (1969) describes the struggle in Susan between a drive to grow—a "creative fury"—and an opposing tendency towards "a merely compliant adaptation" (p. 431), as a struggle from which the analyst cannot stay out, because creative surrender is accomplished through becoming a pliable medium. The latter provides a way for the patient to express how he or she feels about a specific healing factor in his or her analysis, namely, having found a piece of the external world that can be safely treated as a piece of the self, and can thus be used as a bridge between inside and outside. Indeed, for some patients it is necessary to discover that their therapists are really what they think they are in the transference situation (Milner, 1949). That is, it is necessary for them to go through a phase of relationship with the therapist in which the latter supports the patient's primary illusion of omnipotence (Milner, 1952b, 1956a). From the therapist's point of view this means allowing him/herself to be more of an 'instrument' than a 'creator,' leaving this function to the patients themselves.

In other words, according to Milner (1969) "no-one in this kind of work can ever cure another but only help to release the self-curing forces" (p. 317). The therapist should become the servant of a process that works for the patient's self-cure. To help the patient develop (independently but not alone) this capacity for 'self-cure,' even a seemingly 'minor' technical choice, such as asking the patient for the best words for him or her to describe what he or she is feeling, actually has much greater significance. It means acknowledging to the patient the power of the analysis of her own experiences and her internal and external realities, restoring to her the right to fantasize that early adaptation and family intrusions had damaged. Only after a long period of processing her suspicion of Milner could Susan talk to her about intense and wonderful feelings and distressing feelings, and add that however terrible some of those feelings are, they are worth sharing, because for the first time she feels herself.

Encountering a 'pliable medium' can change the internal environment of those patients whose structuring took place in having to adapt to a family environment that was not good enough, so it had been necessary for them to enact early ego development as a controlling defense function with respect to their family and social life events (e.g., parenting dynamics, separations, the war, etc.).

In Milner's technical choices, it emerges clearly how the clinician's intentionality was allowed to overlap with the creative contribution of the subject—victim of clinical zeal—thus putting it in a shadow zone and making it unthinkable. Milner retrospectively understands that one should not try to 'cure' anyone with psychoanalysis, and that the attachment of some patients to their symptoms may be, at least in part, a protest against the therapist's tendency to pursue the belief that she can cure (i.e., change) them. It is the tendency "to do too much for [the patient] and to interpret too much in terms of the 'good object,' not taking enough account of the 'good subject'" (Milner, 1969, p. 442).

An experiential point of arrival

The journey taken with Susan acquires a meaning that moves out of the framework of nosography and treatment theory and into a more reflective dimension, into the horizon of what is 'culture.' Milner questions the usefulness of considering all the phases of thinking in which the subject does not distinguish between the seer and the seen (i.e., reverie phenomena) as symptoms, something to be disposed of, or—in our culture, so prone to objectivity—to recognize them as something usable in the appropriate place. When in a healthy enough environment, the child can behave and act under the influence of illusions, play 'pretend,' and lose himself in his game feeling, in those moments, that it is reality. Adults, on the other hand, have more difficulty finding contexts that allow this immersion in illusions. In adult life, pretending is more easily entrusted to others, for example, actors with whom one then partially identifies for the duration of the film. However, safely immersing oneself in illusions can and should become a reality in the analytic setting.

The conclusion of this dialogical path is thus not that of a 'decoding' of a message written in a private language to be deciphered, but the construction of an experience that necessarily requires simultaneously the presence of corporeality, of boundaries and frameworks that are however partially surmountable, of areas of emptiness, of contact and temporary fusion.

A form of corporeal thinking

Milner's considerations on the awareness of one's bodily states within the psychoanalytic setting and their effect on the patient are one of her major technical innovations. Milner realizes that her reflection on Susan must have a deeply physical aspect because what she says is often less important than her bodily-mental state in her sessions.

In a kind of rewriting of communicative codes, the analytic work Milner did according to the canons that interpreted transference showed its limitations in the face of several problematic situations: the privacy of such codes, the oddity of various thoughts, the struggle to stand on a more nuanced and descriptive plane, outside the Aristotelian logic with which, for example, Susan seemed to express herself (albeit concretely). Her drawings represent not only a private code, rich in images and concepts also indifferent to the contradictions of logic or to a certain reality testing. They are communications beyond the reach of words used logically and discursively, which tell of how the patient—in this case Susan—may have "had so much, [she] felt so many things, [she] felt in [her] heart and in [her] stomach" (Milner, 1969, p. 12).

It is through drawings that this semiotic system takes space and appears more intensely and meaningfully. Milner interprets Susan's "Catherine wheel" drawing (Milner, 1955, p. 100; Fig. 34 p. 123) in terms of an archaic perception of an inner world where confusion, order, and chaos can be experienced.

> It was as if she were depicting the 'booming, buzzing confusion' of what the inner matrix, the as-yet undifferentiated inner experience of the body, feels like when first faced and out of which crystallizes an image, an impulse or a wish, if this initial chaos can be tolerated.
>
> (p. 106)

Describing Susan's 'concentration in the body' when she draws without knowing what (but also talking about herself in the moments when she voluntarily allows the will to remain at the margins of her creative process), Milner speaks of the rhythmic capacity of the psycho-physical organism. Such psycho-physical capacity can become "a source of order that is more stable than reliance on an order imposed either from outside, or by the planning conscious mind" (Milner, 1957, p. 187). But concentration in the body is also that of the analyst, as she looks at the patient's drawings. Here, Milner takes up and extends to the corporeal the contribution of Jung, who approached the drawings of his adult patients with such focus and attention as to bring about a lowering of attention that makes it possible to capture the 'feeling-tone' or atmosphere of a drawing and its impact upon us. This is a type of tuning that makes it possible to take in what is presented by the unconscious of the person drawing.

As in several other passages in her clinical descriptions, Milner does not pull out of the relationship with her patients but places herself within the framework of their encounter and experiences, both personal and shared. Moreover, she emphasizes how the analyst's gaze is the primary facilitator of the patient's transformative journey. In analyzing Susan's drawings, with the intention of clarifying the larger context in which to place them, Milner discovers in many of them "the presence of aspects of the awareness of an undifferentiated background, whether inner or outer, and the relation of this to the rhythms of bodily experiences" (Milner, 1955, p. 103).

Reference to these bodily experiences opens up considerations of the bodily dimension, the primary context in which it is corporeality that constitutes 'living discourse,' and the proper interpretation of this return from the symbolic and linguistic to the corporeal and non-verbal. Milner (1973) highlights "the importance of the direct non-symbolic internal awareness of one's own body from inside" and shows how "the ongoing background or matrix of one's own sense of being (…) can yet become foreground once one has learnt the skill of directing attention to it" (p. 215).

These references to a corporeality to be read differently appear repeatedly in Milner's work, in reference to both herself (see for example Milner, 1969, p. 102, p. 337) and her patients (see for example p. 40).

Clinical work with certain patients is primarily to allow them a new beginning, but this expression seems likely to lend itself to ambiguity. With Susan, for example, Milner often had the feeling that it was almost as if the patient was claiming that everyone's adult life should always be free of worry and spontaneous, as is that of the newborn to whom the mother provides all the care.

The possibility of experiencing a pliable encounter, with a 'soft' differentiation of boundaries, does not appear to be the result of a regressive desire to go back (a movement that is impossible in time, and therefore pathological), but rather to get back in touch, at least in part, with what had been an obstacle in the past. This new experience can now take place with the adult structure, which also implicitly recalls the impossibility of thinking of a naively understood 'going back.'

Nor is the analyst outside this 'being in the corporeality,' and this becomes an element of the theory of treatment: avoiding the intellectualism of a therapy based on words and not psychophysically embodied. The analyst's body presentation, or direct proprioceptive body-self awareness, should "becomes the foreground of one's consciousness rather than the pre-conscious background" (Milner, 1960, p. 198).

Here Milner enters into territories little trodden by psychoanalysts, such as the function of the self to deliberately learn to relax the whole body, the inability of some patients (see Susan) to feel the weight of the body on the couch or one's feet in contact with the floor, or deliberately directing attention to the various parts of the body in contact with the chair/couch as a way of achieving such relaxation.

Milner's own proceeding is affected. For example, during one session, Milner thinks that Susan's introduction of the theme of the tea is a demonstration of her greater readiness to know that she is reliving aspects of a breastfeeding situation in the here and now of the analytic encounter.

However, Milner does not verbalize anything about it, because she notices the taking shape of a remarkable change in her feelings: she feels connected to her patient in a way she has never experienced before and does not feel the need to smoke.

Central to Milner's formulations are, on the one hand, her observations of changes in the internal perception of one's body over the course of the session (including the effects of deliberately directing one's attention towards the awareness of one's own body) and, on the other hand, the connection between that perception and both creative production and increased emotional involvement with the world around her (including the patient).

Milner also emphasizes another key point. At the same time that space is given to a not-knowing, to a concentration in the body, to pre-verbal communications in which union and fusion can take place, there needs to be the safe certainty that the clinical work does not cause one to remain in a mad state. (A risk that affects both patient and therapist). This is the sense of the communication in which Susan tells Milner (1969, p. 70) that she feels her face is falling apart, and tells her that she is afraid that by falling apart to put herself back together in a new way, she will then not be able to put herself back together in time to go back home at the end of the session.

Frame

We find again here the concept of frame, which becomes the safe space in which one can take the risk of getting in touch with deeper/hidden/anxious parts. In fact, for Milner, identity can only be found and developed in the context of the free expression of personal illusions and stories (Kleimberg, 2023). This paradoxically can only occur within a 'gap' established by frameworks and parameters that invite the patient to search for self and other, and to bridge the gap between internal and external reality (Kleimberg, 2023).

It should be emphasized that, although the therapist comes to see a whole range of possible meanings in the patient's material (drawings, dreams, stories, etc.), it sometimes takes a long time, even years with patients like Susan, before the patient is able to bring them back into the session in a form usable by the analytic couple.

The function of the analytic space is reconfirmed when Susan brings to the session a very significant drawing for both of them

(Milner, 1969, p. 278, Fig. 100), made after ECT nine years earlier, leading Milner to question what had enabled this achievement. The hypothesis formulated by Milner includes two key elements: an increased confidence on the part of Susan that she can be safely held (due in part to positive changes in the extra-analytic environment), and Milner's new position on the need for a state of safety in which it is not necessary to be too constantly aware of separateness.

The dialectic between one-ness and two-ness is thus a key parameter to analyze in order to understand the possibilities for contact and communication in the patient-therapist couple. The therapeutic element of this couple work lies primarily in the experience of shared creativity, within which it is the patient who gives meaning to his or her own experience. Milner had already said those things to the patient, but only now could that vision of Susan's illness be a truly mutual creation. It is a creation, perhaps not too different from that of a parental couple, which, in Milner's conception of emotional development, is necessary for growth towards maturity:

> one cannot grow to being able to love unless one has been adequately loved, by someone, either by parents or parent substitutes, the further idea, one that fits in with psycho-analytic theory; the idea that the task of growing to maturity requires the capacity to set up inside one the fantasy of containing parents who love each other and can be conceived of as creating, in an act of joy and mirth.
>
> (Milner, 1969, p. 449)

Toward an ontological psychoanalysis

The evolution of Susan's treatment highlights how Milner's 'toolbox' has been enriched, by adding to the clinical tools proper to epistemological psychoanalysis, acquired during her training, also those characterizing ontological psychoanalysis. By epistemological psychoanalysis is meant a process of acquiring knowledge and understanding of the patient's unconscious internal world and her relation to the external world, in order to organize the patient's experience in a way that is helpful to her in dealing with her emotional problems and achieving psychic change (Ogden, 2019). The main tools of intervention are transference interpretations in the terms of classic authors such as Freud and Klein, whose purpose is to convey to the patient what is understood of her unconscious fantasies/conflicts/impulses/etc. The use of these interpretations, as well as other 'epistemological tools,' in the early period of Susan's treatment is well described by Milner. On the other hand, ontological psychoanalysis means an approach in which the analyst tends to 'wait' before conveying to the patient what she has understood, where the primary goal is to facilitate the patient's efforts to become more fully him/herself (Ogden, 2019). The pivotal aspect is not the knowledge/understanding reached by the analytic couple, but rather the subjective experience made by the patient in the process of creatively discovering meaning for him/herself and, in this way, becoming more fully him/herself. The clinical tools that allow working in the ontological dimension are, among others, empathy and corporeality, as well as an approach to drawing/playing/dreaming, in which the focus of attention is shifted from symbolic meaning to the experience of doing/observing this. Ogden lists Milner among the thinkers who contributed to the development of the ontological aspects of psychoanalysis, but he places her second to Winnicott and Bion. However, it seems to us that, in light of her contributions and the influence they have had on the thinking of her better-known English colleagues, Milner should be credited with a more prominent role.

Notes

1 In *The Hands of the Living God*, the literal expression "it seems to me" appears 14 times.
2 This note—along with other concepts such as the transitional space, the suppressed madness, the paradoxes of Winnicott, and others—could lead to more articulate elaborations of psychoanalysis as a 'talking cure.'
3 According to Milner, "the outline represented the world of fact, of separate touchable solid objects. To cling to it was therefore surely to protect oneself against the other world, the world of the imagination" (1987, p. 7) in which "no one differentiated from the other, a state of

blissful transcending of boundaries, which, to the conscious ego, would be identified with madness" (1957, p. 182).

4 In recalling these 'situations of exchange'—much beyond just the linguistic plane and of a classically emphasized 'neutrality'—we cannot help but wonder about the theme of the setting, its rules, analytic neutrality, acting... Certainly some clinical sequences are affected by the culture of the time, outside a properly psychoanalytic theory and technique, as in the work with Simon, who was allowed to light a fire in the therapy room. In other material, one is struck by the exchanges between Susan and Milner, which also take place on a plane of great concreteness.

In the absence of a more precise and complete description of the clinical exchanges, we prefer to avoid a kind of 'retrospective supervision' of Milner's possible acts, an aspect of little interest for our work, leaving personal reflections to the reader. These, however, must take into account both the seriousness of Susan's condition (it is therefore the therapist who can and should place himself at the level of best possible communication) and the deeper meaning Milner expresses in her 'not knowing' and creative surrender in the work of the analytic couple.

Taking up a metaphor from Winnicott, if it is true that it is the child who creates meaning where he or she finds it, this is possible only because the breast is placed in the space and time adapted for it to be found. Similarly, it is the therapist who must bring himself to a good enough distance so that, while differentiated, she can be found and utilized.

Chapter 6

Contemporary pliability

This chapter proposes a rereading of Milner's work and writings, to read some of the theoretical and methodological paradigms underlying his work through contemporary eyes, both from a more psychoanalytic point of view and from a more general anthropological and epistemological perspective. A retrospective look allows one to recognize how some of Milner's underlying ideas still have a high degree of 'usability,' still relevant, if not even anticipatory, with respect to a society whose characteristics would only become apparent decades later.

Coming to the end of this book and building on the reflections set forth in the previous chapters on specific theoretical-clinical aspects introduced or used by Marion Milner, set forth in the previous chapter, we now wish to briefly present some non-conclusive considerations that bear witness to the retained relevance of her thought, which because of its pliable nature makes a plurality of readings possible. The focus here is no longer on the individual theoretical concepts proposed by Milner, but on a system of dimensions derived from a metatheoretical reflection that seems useful and fertile within contemporary Western culture.

Search for what is missing. A fundamental task of both the psychoanalyst and the patient within the psychoanalytic encounter is to recognize gaps in their own self-knowledge—also describable as bits of nothingness or inner unknown—, enter into a relationship with them, and achieve an unstructured awareness of all that is behind their most conscious perceptions. Only with the

DOI: 10.4324/9781003330332-7

recognition of these gaps can there be space for a truly transformative evolution.

The richness of bodily experience. The body is a carrier of knowledge beyond the reach of words used or discursively organized in a logical-rational way. During the analytic encounter, the therapist's words are often less important than their psychophysical presence, that is, a kind of deliberate suffusing of their entire body (not just the head, which is a rational-logical thought) with their own consciousness. This body-concentration is a particular type of contemplative and deliberate focus able to enrich the outer reality of certain qualities matching those of the observing subject.

Doubt and observe oneself and others. When in the analytic room, it is important for the analyst to be able to doubt everything they have been taught and try to learn more directly through their senses and less through rational thinking. They will discover that there are different ways of perceiving their experience and that these ways provide them with different facts. That is, each of the different ways of perceiving directs knowledge in a specific different way. It is a position of observation from where the analyst is 'forced' to question their own knowledge and central position. It is a position that questions one's own knowledge and centrality. Through the renunciation of preconstituted knowledge—sometimes perhaps even ideological—there manifests openness to the encounter with the non-me.

Move on and across boundaries. The ability to move on and across boundaries is made possible by the experiences of psychological separation and distance achieved through variations in the feeling of the existence–nonexistence continuum of the body boundary. Art creations, drawings (see Susan's), and communications, in general, are a kind of bridge toward the subject's acceptance of the otherness of the external world. By virtue of having a concrete existence in the external world and, at the same time, an origin and existence in the inner world of the subject who created them, they are a non-discursive affirmation of the subject's reality. Certainly, there is the fear of being crazy, of losing all sense of separating boundaries between what is tangible (the external world) and what is imaginary (the inner world), but it is a 'madness' that arises from a primary state of experience in which the two realities are not distinguished. A state that everyone has lived through during infancy and to which at times one can return. If this return is temporary in nature, then it is not a phase of alienation or collapse but a different way of being and perceiving.

Life as a creative process. Whereas until the mid-twentieth century the creative moment had been regarded as a fragment within a more ordinary everyday life, with Milner's contribution the situation is reversed: it is the ability to be creative that characterizes being alive in a healthy way. What the creative subject embodies in nonverbal symbols are the experiences related to being alive and known from inside, to being a living and moving body in space, capable of relating to other objects. The creative process is part of being alive. What the subject creates is the ability to visualize from the outside what is inside them. The world we see exists because we are able to see it: "the substance of experience is what we bring to what we see" (Milner, 1950, p. 33).

Find common ground. By not needing to cling to the distinction between self and others, the unconscious mind has greater freedom of movement than the conscious logical mind and can swing rhythmically between oneness and duplicity. It seeks the familiar in the unfamiliar, which is why it is more sensitive to similarities than to differences between objects. The basic identifications that make it possible to find the familiar in the unfamiliar (to create a symbol) require the subject to tolerate a temporary loss of sense of self, to temporarily give up reassuring, but poorer in emotional coloring, logical-rational thinking. For Milner, the figure of two overlapping circles represents the model of the analytic relationship in which between analyst and patient there is (should be) an area of overlap where there is a partial fusion of experiences, a common ground.

Go beyond. To overcome the risks of pseudo-adaptation, it is necessary to learn to continuously break the established familiar patterns involving logical rational divisions of me–not–me. The analytic relationship should be a space where one can learn how to do this.

Be used. No therapist/analyst can ever cure a patient, but only help them to release and use self-curative forces. This is a very humble position, but entirely necessary so that each patient met can live a life of their own. That is, they can create their own ability to see their way in personal terms. The therapist provides the premises, the setting in which the patient creates their own inner frame of reference, an inner space in which to be mentally creative on their own. The patient is asked to gradually make their personal contribution, according to their own codes and mechanisms of signification.

The historical-anthropological context in which we currently live is characterized by:

- A society that can be defined as 'liquid,' i.e., characterized by entropic movements tending to enactments rather than working through of uncertainties and disorganizations;
- An identity that has been increasingly problematic in its radicalisms that seek rigid boundaries, as well as in its evolutions that raise questions about new definitions;
- A social dimension in which authenticity and personal creativity are played out within dynamics in which homogenization is prevalent;
- A context in which knowledge and corporeality seem to be objects of consumption instead of places of experience;
- An ethical dimension in which paternalism has lost its value in favor of the principle of autonomy and, where possible, cooperative work;
- An increasingly articulate yet private set of languages/idioms, whose interactions seem to increase a confusion of tongues or glossolalia, rather than the ability to encounter and understand others.

On the basis of these premises, it becomes evident how Milner's thought, somewhat left to the discretionary use of the individual, represents a refined and timely contribution to reflections and work on clinical and applied psychoanalysis.

References

Anderson, J. W. (2023). Talking with Marion Milner about Donald W. Winnicott and about herself (1981). In M. Boyle Spelman & J. Raphael-Leff (Eds), *The Marion Milner tradition: Lines of development: Evolution of theory and practice over the decades* (pp. 29–33) Routledge.

Argenton, A. (1996).*Arte e cognizione [Art and cognition].* Raffaello Cortina.

Balint, M. (1932). Charakteranalyse und Neubeginn. *Internationale Zeitschrift für Psychoanalyse*, 20, 54–65, 1934 (Engl. trans. 1952). Character analysis and new beginning. In *Primary love and psychoanalytic technique* (pp. 151–164). Hogarth Press.

Balint, M. (1936). The final goal of psycho-analytic treatment. *International Journal of Psychoanalysis*, 17, 206–216.

Balint, M. (1960). Primary narcissism and primary love. *Psychoanalytic Quarterly*, 29(1), 6–43.

Bartoli, G. (2003). *Scritti di psicologia dell'arte e dell'esperienza estetica [Writings on the psychology of art and aesthetic experience].* Monolite.

Bartoli, G. (2017). Considerations in relation to some research on the possible neural underpinnings linked to visual artworks observation. *PsicoArt*, 7.

Beebe, B., Cohen, P., & Lachmann, F. (2016). *The mother-infant interaction picture book: Origins of attachment.* W. W. Norton & Co.

Beebe, B., Lyons-Ruth, K., Trevarthen, C., & Tronick, E., et al. (2021). *Infant research and psychoanalysis.* Frenis Zero Press.

Benjamin, J. (2004). Beyond doer and done to: An intersubjective view of thirdness. *Psychoanalytic Quarterly*, 73(1), 5–46.

Berenson, B. (1948). *Aesthetics and history in the visual arts.* Pantheon.

Bertolini, M. (1999). L'impronta e il suo destino. *Imago*, 6(3), 195–204.

Bertolini, M. (2001). "Sulla concentrazione e sugli scopi della psicoanalisi". Paper read at a meeting of the Associazione Italiana di Psicoanalisi (AIPsi), Rome, December 16.

Bertolini, M. (2009). "L'impronta". Paper read at a meeting of the Associazione per lo Studio delle Scienze Neuropsichiatriche dell'Infanzia e adolescenza (ASNEA). Monza, May 2.

Bertolini, M. (2016). Essere nel lavorio psicofisico presimbolico. In A. Giannakoulas & F. Bertolini Neri (Eds), *Continuità dell'essere, crollo e oltre il crollo. Sul lavoro di Donald W. Winnicott* (pp. 19–30). FrancoAngeli.

Bion, W. R. (1959–78). *Cogitations.* Karnac, 1992.

Bion, W. R. (1962). A theory of thinking. *International Journal of Psychoanalysis*, 43, 306–310.

Bion, W. R. (1962). *Learning from Experience.* Maresfield Library.

Bion, W. R. (1967). Notes on memory and desire. *Psychoanalytic Forum*, 2, 279–281.

Bion, W. R. (1970). *Attention and interpretation.* Tavistock Publications.

Bion, W. R. (1975–78). *Clinicals seminars and four papers.* The Fleetwood Press, 1987.

Bion, W. R. (1978–80). *Bion in New York and São Paulo.* Clunie Press.

Blair, C. & Raver, C. C. (2012). Child development in the context of adversity: Experiential canalization of brain and behavior. *American Psychologist*, 67(4), 309–318.

Blake, W. (1788). *All religions are one.* Reprinted by Trianon Press, 2010.

Bleger, J. (1967). Psycho-analysis of the psycho-analytic frame. *International Journal of Psychoanalysis* 48(4), 511–519.

Bollas, C. (1983). Expressive Uses of the countertransference. *Contemporary Psychoanalysis*, 19(1), 1–34.

Bollas, C. (1987). *The shadow of the object.* Free Association Books.

Boyle Spelman, M. (2023). Marion Milner: a many-branched psychologist at work: (The Human Problem in Schools). In M. Boyle Spelman & J. Raphael-Leff (Eds), *The Marion Milner tradition: Lines of development: Evolution of theory and practice over the decades* (pp. 188–202). Routledge.

Boyle Spelman, M., & Raphael-Leff, J. (Eds) (2023). *The Marion Milner tradition: Lines of development: Evolution of theory and practice over the decades.* Routledge.

Breton, A. (1972). *Manifestes Du Surréalisme* [1924]. University of Michigan Press.

Britton, R., Chused, J., Ellman, S., Ellman, C., & Likierman, M. (2006). Panel II: The oedipus complex, the primal scene, and the superego. *Journal of Infant, Child & Adolescent Psychotherapy*, 5, 282–307.

Britton, R. (2015). *Between mind and brain: Models of the mind and models in the mind.* Karnac.

Bruggen, P. (2023). 'I was her last Training Case' – analysis with Marion Milner and supervision with Winnicott. (Conversation with Margaret Boyle Spelman: 27th of May 2005; 8th of July 2017). In M. Boyle Spelman & J. Raphael-Leff (Eds), *The Marion Milner Tradition: Lines of Development: Evolution of Theory and Practice over the Decades* (pp. 85–87). Routledge.

Caldwell, L. (2014). Image and process: Psychoanalysis or art? *British Journal of Psychotherapy*, 30(3), 337–348.

Caldwell, L. (2022). 'Milner and the origins of creativity'. From symbolism to symbol formation and illusion. In M. Boyle Spelman & J. Raphael-Leff (Eds), *The Marion Milner Tradition: Lines of Development: Evolution of Theory and Practice over the Decades* (pp. 115–119) Routledge.

Cassullo, G. (2019a). Janet and Freud. Long-time rivals. In G. Craparo, F. Ortu and O. van der Hart, (Eds). *Rediscovering Pierre Janet. Trauma, Dissociation, and a New Context for Psychoanalysis* (pp. 43–52). Routledge.

Cassullo, G. (2019b). On not taking just one part of it: Janet's influence on object relations theory. In G. Craparo, F. Ortu, & O. van der Hart, (Eds). *Rediscovering Pierre Janet. Trauma, Dissociation, and a New Context for Psychoanalysis* (pp. 66–74). Routledge.

Cassullo, G. & Stefana, A. (2023). Some essential concepts of Marion Blackett Milner. Framing, Concentration, Absentmindedness, Rêverie. In M. Boyle Spelman & J. Raphael-Leff (Eds), *The Marion Milner Tradition: Lines of Development: Evolution of Theory and Practice over the Decades* (pp. 7–13). Routledge.

Caudwell, C. (1937). *Illusion and Reality.* Macmillan.

Chagas Bovet, A. M. (1997). Gioco ed eccitazione. *Richard e Piggle*, 5(2), 191–200.

Chagas Bovet, A. M. (1999). Visitando i percorsi dell'illusione. *Richard e Piggle*, 7(2), 143–152.

Coburn, C., Featherstone, W., Jeffs, A., & Shafer, A. (2023). 'What sort of therapist are you?' Reflections on the suppressed madness of sane men. In M. Boyle Spelman & J. Raphael-Leff (Eds), *The Marion Milner Tradition: Lines of Development: Evolution of Theory and Practice over the Decades* (pp. 213–218). Routledge.

Coleridge S. T. (1817). *Biographia literaria: Or biographical sketches of my literary life and opinions.*

Damasio, A. (2010). *Self comes to mind.* Heinemann Dawkins.

Dewey, J. (1934). *Art as experience*. G. P. Putnam's Sons.

Di Benedetto, A. (1991a). Countertransference: feeling, recreating and understanding. *Rivista di Psicoanalisi*, 37, 94–130.

Di Benedetto, A. (1991b). Listening to the pre-verbal: the beginning of the affects. *Rivista di Psicoanalisi*, 37, 400–426.

Dimitrijević, A. (2023). Series editor's introduction. In M. Boyle Spelman & J. Raphael-Leff (Eds), *The Marion Milner Tradition: Lines of Development: Evolution of Theory and Practice over the Decades* (pp. xxv–xxvi). Routledge.

Dragstedt, N. R. (1998). Creative illusions: The theoretical and clinical work of Marion Milner. *Journal of Melanie Klein and Object Relations*, 16(3), 425–536.

Dutton, D. (2010). *The art instinct: Beauty, pleasure, and human evolution*. Bloomsbury.

Eco, U. (1962). *Opera aperta*. Bompiani.

Eco, U. (2004). *History of Beauty*. Rizzoli.

Eco, U. (2007). *On ugliness*. Rizzoli.

Ehrenzweig, A. (1953). *The psycho-analysis of artistic vision and hearing*. Routledge and Kegan Paul.

Ehrenzweig, A. (1957). The creative surrender: A comment on Joanna Field's book An Experiment in Leisure. *American Imago*, 14(3), 193–210.

Eigen, M. (1977). On working with unwanted patients. *International Journal of Psychoanalysis*, 58(1), 109–121.

Eigen, M. (1983). Dual union or undifferentiation? A critique of Marion Milner's view of the sense of psychic creativeness. *International Review of Psycho-Analysis*, 10(4), 415–428.

Eigen, M. (2015). O, orgasm and beyond. *Psychoanalytical Dialagues*, 25, 646–654.

Eigen M. (2023). The use creativity can make of pain. In M. Boyle Spelman & J. Raphael-Leff (Eds), *The Marion Milner tradition: Lines of development: evolution of theory and practice over the decades* (pp. 27–28). Routledge.

Eliot, T. S. (1936). Burnt Norton. In *Four quartets*. Harcourt, Brace & Co., 1943.

Faimberg, H. (2018). José Bleger and the relevance today of his dialectical frame. In Tylim, I. & Harris, A. (Eds), *Reconsidering the moveable frame in psychoanalysis: Its function and structure in contemporary psychoanalytic theory* (pp. 40–54). Routledge.

Featherstone, W. (2023). A deeper-rooted kind of knowing. In M. Boyle Spelman & J. Raphael-Leff (Eds), *The Marion Milner tradition: Lines of development: evolution of theory and practice over the decades* (pp. 153–163). Routledge.

Ferenczi, S. (1913). Stages in the development of the sense of reality. In *Selected writings*. Penguin, 1999.

Freud, S. (1899). The interpretation of dreams. *The Standard Edition of the Complete Psychological Works of Sigmund Freud*, Vols 4, 5, ix–627.

Freud, S. (1906). Delusions and dreams in Jensen's Gradiva. *S.E.*, Vol. 9, 3–95.

Freud, S. (1910). Leonardo da Vinci and a memory of his childhood. *S.E.*, Vol. 11, 59–137.

Freud, S. (1913). The claims of psycho-analysis to scientific interest. *S.E.*, Vol. 13, 163–190.

Freud, S. (1914). On Narcissism: An introduction. *S.E.*, Vol. 14, 76–77.

Freud, S. (1915). Instincts and their vicissitudes. *S.E.*, Vol. 14, 111–140.

Freud, S. (1917) Introductory lectures on psycho-analysis. *S.E.*, Vol. 16, 448–463.

Freud, S. (1925). Inhibition, symptoms and anxiety. *S.E.*, Vol. 20, 77–115.

Freud, S. (1929). Civilization and its discontents. *S.E.*, Vol. 21, 57–146.

Freud, S. (1932). New introductory lectures on psychoanalysis. *S.E.*, Vol. 22, 1–182.

Freud, S. (1938). Letter from Sigmund Freud to Stefan Zweig, July 20. In *The letters of Sigmund Freud and Arnold Zweig*. Hogarth Press and the Institute of Psycho-Analysis, 1970.

Giannakoulas, A. (2010). La follia rimossa della coppia sana. *Psicobiettivo*, 2, 48–65.

Giannakoulas, A. (2023). 'My analyst Marion Milner'. In M. Boyle Spelman & J. Raphael-Leff (Eds), *The Marion Milner tradition: Lines of development: Evolution of theory and practice over the decades* (pp. 78–82). Routledge.

Giannakoulas, A. & Hernandez, M. (2010). Rimembrare la mente e rammentare il corpo. *Psicoanalisi*, 14, 69–81.

Glover, N. (2009). *Psychoanalytic aesthetics: An introduction to the British School*. Karnac.

Gombrich, E. H. (1954). Psycho-analysis and the history of art. *International Journal of Psychoanalysis*, 35(4), 401–411.

Gombrich, E. H. (1987). *Reflections on the history of art: views and reviews*. Phaidon.

Gorer, G. (1970). The hands of the living God. *International Journal of Psychoanalysis*, 51, 533–534.

Green, A. (1977). La royauté appartient à l'enfant. *L'arc*, 69, 4–12.

Green, A. (2011). *Illusions and disillusions of psychoanalytic work*. Karnac Books.

Grinberg, L. (1979). Countertransference and projective counter-identification. *Contemporary Psychoanalysis*, 15(2), 226–247.

Grosskurth, P. (1986). *Melanie Klein: Her world and her work*. Knopf.

Hagman, G. (2005). *Aesthetic experience: Beauty, creativity, and the search for the ideal*. Rodopi.

Haughton, H. (2011). Introduction. In M. Milner, *Eternity's sunrise: A way of keeping a diary* (pp. xi–xxxiii). Routledge.

Haughton, H. (2014). The Milner experiment: Psychoanalysis and the diary. *British Journal of Psychology*, 3, 349–362.

Hernandez, M. (2015). "Mario Bertolini: il going on being dell'analista nel setting." Paper read at a meeting of the Associazione Italiana di Psicoanalisi (AIPsi), Monza, April 16.

Hernandez, M. & Giannakoulas, A. (1997). On the costruction of potential space. In M. Bertolini, A. Giannakoulas, & M. Hernandez (Eds). *Squiggles and spaces* (pp. 146–163), Vol. 1. Whurr, 2001.

Hinshelwood, R. D. (1989). *A Dictionary of Kleinian thought*. Free Association Books.

Hughes, J. M. (1989). *Reshaping the psychoanalytic domain: The work of Melanie Klein, W. R. D. Fairbairn, and D. W. Winnicott*. University of California Press.

Imbasciati, A. (2006). *Constructing a mind*. Routledge.

Janet, P. (1889). *L'automatisme psychologique*. Felix Alcan.

Jones, E. (1918). The theory of symbolism. *British Journal of Psychology*, 9, 181–229.

Johnston, G. (2016). Queer lives. wilde, sackville-west, and woolf. In A. Smyth (Ed.), *A History of English autobiography* (pp. 269–283). Cambridge University Press.

Jordan, J. F. (1990). Inner space and the interior of the maternal body: Unfolding in the psychoanalytical process. *International Review of Psychoanalysis*, 17, 433–444.

Jung, C. G. (1916). The transcendent function. *Collected works of C.G. Jung, Vol. 8.*

Jung, C. G. (1921). Psychological types. *Collected works of C.G. Jung, Vol. 6.*

Kandinsky, W. (1914). *The art of spiritual harmony*. Cosimo, 2007.

Keats, J. (1895). *The letters of John Keats*. Kessinger Publishing, 2004.

Khan, M. M. R. (1960). Clinical aspects of the schizoid personality: affects and technique. *International Journal of Psychoanalysis*, 41(3), 430–436.

Khan, M. M. R. (1963). The concept of cumulative trauma. *The Psychoanalytic Study of the Child*, 18(1), 286–306.

Khan, M. M. R. (1971). The Role of Illusion in the analytic space and process. *Annual of Psychoanalysis*, 1, 231–246.

Khan, M. M. R. (1977). On lying fallow. In *Hidden selves* (pp. 183–188). Maresfield Library, 1989.

Kleimberg, L. (2019). Dramatización ilusoria. La ficción entre la verdad material y la verdad histórica [Illusory dramatization. The fiction between material truth and historical truth]. *Revista Peruana de Psicoanálisis*, 24, 73–89.

Kleimberg, L. (2023). 'A meaningful encounter' – my supervision with Marion Milner (1990–1993). In M. Boyle Spelman & J. Raphael-Leff (Eds), *The Marion Milner tradition: Lines of development: Evolution of theory and practice over the decades* (pp. 98–99). Routledge.

Klein, M. (1923). The development of a child. *International Review of Psycho-Analysis*, 4, 419–474.

Klein, M. (1926). Infant analysis [1923]. *International Journal of Psychoanalysis*, 7, 31–63.

Klein, M. (1929). Infantile anxiety-situations reflected in a work of art and in the creative impulse. *International Journal of Psychoanalysis*, 10, 436–443.

Klein, M. (1930). The importance of symbol-formation in the development of the ego. *International Journal of Psychoanalysis*, 11, 24–39.

Klein, M. (1946). Notes on some schizoid mechanisms. *International Journal of Psychoanalysis*, 27, 99–110.

Klein, M. (1948). *Contributions to psychoanalysis, 1921–1945*. Hogarth Press.

Klein, M. (1957). *Envy and gratitude; a study of unconscious sources*. Basic Books.

Klein, M. (1958). On the development of mental functioning. *International Journal of Psychoanalysis*, 39(2–4),84–90.

Klein, M. (1959). Our adult world and its roots in infancy. In *Our adult world and other essays*. Heinemann Medical Books.

Klein, M. (1960). Some reflections on the Oresteia. In *Our adult world and other essays*. Heinemann Medical Books.

Kluzer Usuelli, A. (1992). The significance of illusion in the work of Freud and Winnicott: A controversial issue. *International Review of Psycho-Analysis*, 19(2), 179–187.

Kohon, G. (2016). *Reflections on the aesthetic experience: Psychoanalysis and the uncanny*. Routledge.

Krieger, M. (1976). *Theory of criticism*. John Hopkins University Press.

Kris, E. (1952). *Psychoanalytic explorations in art*. International Universities Press.

Langer, K. S. (1942). *Philosophy in a new key*. Harvard University Press.

Langer, K. S. (1953). *Feeling and form*. Ch. Scribner's Sons.

Lavelli, M., Stefana, A., Lee, S. H., & Beebe, B. (2022). Preterm infant contingent communication in the neonatal intensive care unit with mothers versus fathers. *Developmental Psychology*, 58(2), 270–285.

Letley, E. (2013). *Marion Milner: The life*. Routledge.

Maclagan, D. (1992). Between psychoanalysis and surrealism: the collaboration between Grace Pailthorpe and Reuben Mednikoff. *Free Associations*, 3, 33–50.

Maclagan, D. (2001). *Psychological Aesthetics: Painting, feeling and making sense*. Jessica Kingsley Publishers.

Magritte, R. (1938). Lifeline. In M. A. Caws (Ed.), *Surrealist painters and poets: an antology*. MIT Press, 2002.

Malleson, A. (2023). 'Marion was uniquely placed to understand'... (analyses with Marion Milner and with Donald Winnicott). In M. Boyle Spelman & J. Raphael-Leff (Eds), *The Marion Milner tradition: Lines of development: Evolution of theory and practice over the decades* (pp. 88–94). Routledge.

Maritain, J. (1953). *Creative intuition in art and poetry*. Pantheon Books.

Marks, L. (2014). Creative surrender: A Milnerian view of works by Y. Z. Kami. *International Journal of Psychoanalysis*, 95(1), 67–81.

Mayo, E. (1924). *Revery and industrial fatigue*. Williams & Wilkins.

Milner, M. (1934). *A life of one's own*. Chatto & Windus.

Milner, M. (1937). *An experiment in leisure*. Chatto & Windus.

Milner, M. (1938). *The human problem in schools. A psychological study carried out on behalf of the girls' public day school trust*. Methuen & Co Ltd (reprinted by Routledge, 2021).

Milner, M. (1942). The child's capacity for doubt. In *The suppressed madness of sane men* (pp. 9–11). Institute of Psycho-Analysis-Tavistock Publications Ltd, 1987.

Milner, M. (1944). A suicidal symptom in a child of 3. In *The suppressed madness of sane men* (pp. 16–28). Institute of Psycho-Analysis-Tavistock Publications Ltd, 1987.

Milner, M. (1945) Some aspects of phantasy in relation to general psychology. In *The suppressed madness of sane men* (pp. 29–46). Institute of Psycho-Analysis-Tavistock Publications Ltd.

Milner, M. (1948). An adult patient uses toys. In *The suppressed madness of sane men* (pp. 50–54). Institute of Psycho-Analysis-Tavistock Publications Ltd, 1987.

Milner, M. (1949). The ending of two analysis. In *The suppressed madness of sane men* (pp. 55–58). Institute of Psycho-Analysis-Tavistock Publications Ltd, 1987.

Milner, M. (1950). *On not being able to paint*. Heinemann (reprinted by Routledge, 2010).

Milner, M. (1952a). The framed gap. In *The suppressed madness of sane men* (pp. 59–61). Institute of Psycho-Analysis, 1987.

Milner, M. (1952b). Aspects of symbolism in comprehension of the not-self. *International Journal of Psychoanalysis*, 33(2), 181–195.

Milner, M. (1952c). The role of illusion in symbol formation. In *The suppressed madness of sane men* (pp. 62–84). Institute of Psycho-Analysis-Tavistock Publications Ltd, 1987.

Milner, M. (1955). The communication of primary sensual experience—(The Yell of Joy). In *The suppressed madness of sane men* (pp. 85–136). Institute of Psycho-Analysis-Tavistock Publications Ltd, 1987.

Milner, M. (1956a). Psychoanalysis and art. In *The suppressed madness of sane men* (pp. 156–180). Institute of Psycho-Analysis-Tavistock Publications Ltd, 1987.

Milner, M. (1956b). The sense in nonsense: Freud and Blake's job. In *The suppressed madness of sane men* (pp. 137–155). Institute of Psycho-Analysis-Tavistock Publications Ltd, 1987.

Milner, M. (1957). The ordering of chaos. In *The suppressed madness of sane men* (pp. 181–193). Institute of Psycho-Analysis-Tavistock Publications Ltd, 1987.

Milner, M. (1960). The concentration of the body. In *The suppressed madness of sane men* (pp. 194–199). Institute of Psycho-Analysis-Tavistock Publications Ltd, 1987.

Milner, M. (1969). *The hands of the living god*. Hogarth Press (reprinted by Routledge, 2010).

Milner, M. (1977). Winnicott and overlapping circles. In *The suppressed madness of sane men* (pp. 228–233). Institute of Psycho-Analysis-Tavistock Publications Ltd, 1987.

Milner, M. (1973). Some notes on psychoanalytic ideas about mysticism. In *The suppressed madness of sane men* (pp. 258–274). Institute of Psychoanalysis-Tavistock Publications Ltd, 1987.

Milner, M. (1987b). *Eternity's sunrise*. Virago.

Milner, M. (2012). *Bothered by alligators*. Routledge.

Mitchell, S. A. (2000). *Relationality: From attachment to intersubjectivity*. Routledge, 2014.

Mitchell J. (2023). Marion Milner. Thinking together… (on her supervision with Milner 1977–1978). In M. Boyle Spelman & J. Raphael-

Leff (Eds), *The Marion Milner tradition: Lines of development: Evolution of theory and practice over the decades* (pp. 95–97) Routledge.

Montanaro, L. A. & Stefana, A. (2024,). *Surrealism and psychoanalysis in Grace Pailthorpe's life and work.* Routledge

Ogden, T. H. (1994). *Subjects of analysis.* Aronson.

Ogden, T. H. (1997). Reconsidering three aspects of psychoanalytic technique. *International Journal of Psychoanalysis,* 77, 883–899.

Ogden, T. H. (2005). *This art of psychoanalysis.* Routledge.

Ogden, T. H. (2016). Destruction reconceived: on Winnicott's 'The use of an object and relating through identifications'. *International Journal of Psychoanalysis,* 97(5), 1243–1262.

Ogden, T. H. (2018). How I talk with my patients. *Psychoanalytic Quarterly,* 87(3), 399–413.

Ogden, T. H. (2019). Ontological psychoanalysis or "What do you want to be when you grow up?". *Psychoanalytic Quarterly,* 88(4), 661–684.

Panofsky, E. (1955). *The meaning in the visual arts.* Doubleday.

Peterfreund, E. (1978). Some critical comments on psychoanalytic conceptualizations of infancy. *International Journal of Psychoanalysis,* 59 (4), 427–441.

Phillips, A. (2023). My friend, Marion Milner. In M. Boyle Spelman & J. Raphael-Leff (Eds), *The Marion Milner tradition: Lines of development: Evolution of theory and practice over the decades* (pp. 61–68). Routledge.

Pinotti, A. (2010). Quasi-soggetti e come-se: l'empatia nell'esperienza artistica. *PsicoArt,* 1, 1–21.

Raphael-Leff, J. (2023). 'Access to darkly hidden powers'—the context to Marion Milner's psychoanalytic training and clinical work. In M. Boyle Spelman & J. Raphael-Leff (Eds), *The Marion Milner tradition: Lines of development: Evolution of theory and practice over the decades* (pp. 72–77). Routledge.

Rank, O. (1932). *Art and artist.* Knopf.

Rayner, E. (1991). *The independent mind in British psycho-analysis.* Free Association.

Read, H. (1951). Psycho-analysis and the problem of aesthetic value. *International Journal of Psychoanalysis,* 32(2), 73–82.

Reid, S. (1997). *Developments in infant observation. The Tavistock model.* Routledge.

Rodman, F. R. (Ed.) (1993). *The spontaneous gesture: Selected letters of D. W. Winnicott.* Karnac.

Rodman, F. R. (2003). *Winnicott: Life and work.* Perseus Publishing.

Rolland, R. (1927). Letter from Rolland to Freud, 5 December 1927, Cahier 17. *Un Beau Visage à tous sens. Choix de lettres de Romain Rolland (1866–1944)* pp. 264–266. Albin Michel, 1967.

Santayana, G. (1920). *Little essays.* Constable.

Sayers, J. (2002). Marion Milner, mysticism and psycho-analysis. *International Journal of Psychoanalysis*, 83(1), 105–120.

Schaverien, J. (1997). Transference and transactional objects in the treatment of psychosis. In J. Schaverien and K. Killick (Eds), *Art psychotherapy and psychosis* (pp. 13–37). Routledge.

Scott, J (2023). 'Jugs, Mugs, and Goblets', Comments on Marion Milner's artistic insights. In M. Boyle Spelman & J. Raphael-Leff (Eds), *The Marion Milner tradition: Lines of development: Evolution of theory and practice over the decades* (pp. 138–144). Routledge.

Segal, H. (1950). Some aspect of the analysis of a schizophrenic. *International Journal of Psychoanalysis*, 31, 268–278.

Segal, H. (1952). A psychoanalytic approach to aesthetics. *International Journal of Psychoanalysis*, 33(2), 196–207.

Sharpe, E. F. (1935). Similar and divergent unconscious determinants underlying the sublimations of pure art and pure science. *International Journal of Psychoanalysis*, 6, 186–202.

Silberer, J. (1909). Report on a method of eliciting and observing certain symbolic hallucination-phenomena. In D. Rapaport (Ed.), *Organization and pathology of thought: Selected sources* (pp. 195–207). Columbia University Press, 1951.

Speed, H. (1913). *The practice and science of drawing.* Seeley, Service & Co.

Spillius, E.B., Milton, J., Garvey, P., Couve, C., & Steiner, D. (2011). *The new dictionary of Kleinian thought.* Routledge.

Spitz, E. H. (1985). *Art and psyche.* Yale University Press.

Spitz E. H. (2012). Psychoanalysis and the visual arts. In G. O. Gabbard, B. E. Litowitz, & P. Williams (Eds), *The textbook of psychoanalysis, Second edition* (pp. 523–535). American Psychiatric Publishing.

Spitz, E. H. (2016). *Psychoanalysis and the visual arts.* Routledge.

Stefana A. (2011). Introduzione al pensiero di Marion Milner [Introduction to Marion Milner's thought]. *Psicoterapia e Scienze Umane*, XLV (3), 355–374.

Stefana, A. (2014). Marion Milner e il passaggio dall'oggetto primario all'oggetto secondario [Marion Milner: the transition from the primary object to the secondary object]. *Richard e Piggle*, 22(3), 288–301.

Stefana, A. (2015). The origins of the notion of countertransference. *Psychoanalytic Review*, 102(4), 437–460.

Stefana, A. (2017). *History of Countertransference. From Freud to the British Object Relations School*. Routledge.

Stefana, A. (2018). From *Die Traumdeutung* to *The squiggle game*: A brief history of an evolution. *American Journal Psychoanalysis*, 72(1), 182–194.

Stefana, A. (2019). Revisiting Marion Milner's work on creativity and art. *International Journal of Psychoanalysis*, 100(1), 128–147.

Stefana, A. & Gamba, A. (2018). From 'squiggle game' to 'reciprocity game'. For a creative co-construction of a working space with adolescents. *International Journal of Psychoanalysis*, 99(2), 355–379.

Stefana, A., Hinshelwood, R. D., & Borensztejn, C. L. (2021). Racker and Heimann on countertransference: Similarities and differences. *Psychoanalytic Quarterly*, 90(1), 105–137.

Stefana, A., Lavelli, M., Rossi, G., & Beebe, B. (2020). Interactive sequences between fathers and preterm infants in the neonatal intensive care unit. *Early Human Development*, 140, 104888.

Stefana, A. & Montanaro, L. A. (Eds) (2022). *Grace Pailthorpe's writings on psychoanalysis and Surrealism*. Routledge.

Stern, D. N. (1985). *The interpersonal world of the infant*. Basic.

Stern, D. N. (1998). Non-interpretative mechanisms in psychoanalytic therapy. *International Journal of Psychoanalysis*, 79(5), 903–921.

Stern, D. N. & Boston Change Process Study Group. (2005). The something more than interpretation revisited. *Journal of American Psychoanalytical Association*, 53(3), 693–729.

Stokes A. (1955). Form in art. In M. Klein, P. Heimann, & R. Money-Kyrle (Eds), *New directions in psycho-analysis* (pp. 406–420). Tavistock.

Tan, E. S. (2000). Emotion, art and the humanities. In M. Lewis, & J. M. Haviland-Jones (Eds), *Handbook of Emotions*, 2nd ed. (pp. 116–136). Guilford Press.

Tomlin, A. (2008). Introduction: Contemplating the undefinable. In R. Shusterman & A. Tomlin (Eds), *Aesthetic experience* (pp. 1–13). Routledge.

Tronick, E. Z. & Weinberg, M. K. (1997). Depressed mothers and infants: Failure to form dyadic states of consciousness. In L. Murray & P. J. Cooper (Eds), *Postpartum depression and child development* (pp. 54–81). Guilford Press.

Turner, J. F. (2002). A brief history of illusion. *International Journal of Psychoanalysis*, 83(5), 1063–1082.

Tustin, F. (1994) The perpetuation of an error. *Journal of Child Psychotherapy* 20(1), 3–23.

Vallino, D. & Macciò, M. (2004). *Essere neonati*. Borla.

Vischer, R. (1873). *Über das optische Formgefühl: ein Beiträg zur Ästhetik*. Credner.

Walsh, N. & Wilson, A. (1998). *See sluice gates of the mind: The collaborative work of Pailthorpe and Mednikoff*. Leeds Museums and Galleries.

Walters, M. (2012). Introduction. In M. Milner, *Bothered by alligators* (pp. xi–xxii). Routledge.

Winnicott, D. W. (1941). The observation of infants in a set situation. *International Journal of Psychoanalysis*, 22, 229–249.

Winnicott, D. W. (1945). Primitive emotional development. *International Journal of Psychoanalysis*, 26, 137–143.

Winnicott, D. W. (1949). Hate in countertransference. *International Journal of Psychoanalysis*, 30, 69–74.

Winnicott D. W. (1950). Aggression in relation to emotional development. In *Through Paediatrics to Psychoanalysis*. Tavistock, 1958.

Winnicott, D. W. (1951). Critical notice of *On not Being Able to Paint* by Marion Milner. In C. Winnicott, R. Shepherd, & M. Davis (Eds), *Psychoanalytic Explorations* (pp. 390–392). Karnac, 1989.

Winnicott D. W. (1953). Transitional objects and transitional phenomena. *International Journal of Psychoanalysis*, 34(2), 89–97.

Winnicott, D. W. (1954). Mind and its relation to the psyche-soma. *British Journal of Medical Psychology*, 27(4), 201–209.

Winnicott, D. W. (1955). Metapsychological and clinical aspects of regression within the psycho-analytical set-up. *International Journal of Psychoanalysis*, 36(1), 16–26.

Winnicott, D. W. (1956). Primary maternal preoccupation. In *Collected Papers: Through Paediatrics to Psycho-Analysis*. Basic Books.

Winnicott, D. W. (1958). The capacity to be alone. In *The maturational processes and the facilitating environment: Studies in the theory of emotional development* (pp. 29–36). Karnac Books.

Winnicott, D. W. (1962) Ego Integration and Child Development. In *The maturational processes and the facilitating environment: Studies in the theory of emotional development* (pp. 56–63). Karnac Books.

Winnicott, D. W. (1963). The development of the capacity for concern. *Bulletin of the Menninger Clinic*, 27, 167–176.

Winnicott, D. W. (1967). Mirror-role of mother and family in child development. In *Playing and reality* (pp. 111–118). Hogarth Press, 1971.

Winnicott, D. W. (1968). The squiggle game. In *Psycho-analytic explorations*. Harvard University Press, 1989.

Winnicott, D. W. (1969) The use of an object. *International Journal of Psychoanalysis* 50(4), 711–716.

Winnicott D. W. (1970). Individuation. In *Psychoanalytic explorations* (pp. 284–288). Harvard University Press.

Winnicott, D.W. (1971a). *Therapeutic consultation in child psychiatry.* Hogarth Press.

Winnicott, D.W. (1971b). *Playing and reality.* Hogarth Press.

Wordsworth, W. (1800). Preface. In W. Wordsworth & S. T. Coleridge, *Lyrical ballads* (1798). *Broadview Editions,* 2008.

Index

Printed and bound by CPI Group (UK) Ltd, Croydon, CR0 4YY

10/07/2024

01017552-0002